WHAT WE BELIEVE

LEADER'S GUIDE • PART 1
SECOND EDITION

CRC Publications
Grand Rapids, Michigan

Cover photo: SW Productions/PhotoDisc

We welcome your comments. Call us at 1-800-333-8300 or e-mail us at editors@crcpublications.org.

ISBN 1-56212-527-3

10 9 8 7 6 5 4 3 2 1

Contents

Introduction

You are reading the leader's guide to Part One (sessions 1-12) of a twenty-four–session video course entitled *What We Believe*.

When we first produced *What We Believe* back in 1988, we thought it would serve the churches well for perhaps five years or so. To our delight, demand for the course far surpassed our predictions and remains strong today. Thousands of students and many leaders have watched the video and used these materials to learn or review the basics of our faith.

In response to numerous requests to "update" this popular course, CRC Publications, with the help of Back to God Hour television, persuaded Rev. Lew Vander Meer to re-shoot the video. We've added many fresh ideas and examples as well as a number of scenes shot outside the studio. We've revised this leader's guide, adding leader tips, options, and a number of new discussion questions. The student session guides, originally written by Curt Walters, were also revised.

FORMAT AND AUDIENCE

This twenty-four–session course teaches students in grades nine through twelve the basics of the Christian faith according to the Reformed/Presbyterian tradition. Although this is not a course on the Belgic Confession, the sessions basically follow its sequence and frequently refer to its articles (if the Belgic is not part of your confessional tradition, you can omit referring to it during the discussion part of the course).

Each session in this course features a twenty-minute video presentation by Rev. Lew Vander Meer, a veteran high school Bible teacher and pastor. After each video presentation, students use a handout to review key facts, discuss issues raised by the video, and apply the teachings to their lives.

What We Believe may be adapted to various patterns of use. For example, some groups might want to use all twenty-four sessions in sequence in a single year; other groups may prefer to use twelve sessions one year and twelve the following year; still others might take a breather after a dozen sessions, study some other nondoctrinal material for a few weeks, then return to study the remaining twelve sessions. Adjust your own use of these materials to your schedule and to the reactions you hear from your students.

GOALS OF THE COURSE

What We Believe is designed to

- encourage young people to make a commitment to Christ as their personal Savior and Lord.
- help young people understand the systematic structure of Reformed doctrine and enable them to acquire and use a basic "faith vocabulary" common to the Reformed/Presbyterian tradition.
- help young people appreciate the Reformed/Presbyterian tradition of Christianity in comparison with other traditions.
- enable students to see a clear connection between doctrine and life and to respond positively to the teachings of the church.

SESSION GUIDES

A set of twelve revised session guides accompanies each of the two parts of *What We Believe.* The session guides should be torn from the perforated booklet and distributed to the students at the beginning of each session before the video segment is shown. After each session, encourage your students to save their session guides as a summary of the main teachings of the church. (You may want to provide a two-pocket folder as something of an incentive for doing so.) No homework is required or suggested for this course.

Beginning with session 2, each session guide includes a review quiz designed to help students recall key ideas from previous sessions. The quizzes focus primarily on the previous week's video but also include questions on earlier sessions. Answers to all quizzes are given in this guide.

Session guides also include a space for answers to the Bible Trivia questions Pastor Lew asks on the video (evaluations of the original course show that students really enjoyed these questions). Your students can check their own answers against those given by Pastor Lew at the end of each video presentation.

The section called "Video Discussion Guide" offers questions and other activities that review key facts from the video, raise issues for discussion, and draw practical applications. You will need to determine how many of these questions you can handle in your allotted time. We encourage you to supplement (or occasionally replace) our questions with your own or those of your students.

You may want to provide copies of the Belgic Confession for your group; the video refers to and quotes from specific articles of this confession. If you plan to incorporate these references into your discussion of the video, it would be helpful to have at least one copy for every two students. You'll find the Belgic Confession in the back of the *Psalter Hymnal.* It's also available in simple booklet form from CRC Publications.

If your denomination does not use the Belgic Confession, you may, of course, choose not to discuss it during your class sessions. Most of the print references to the Belgic Confession are by way of options that you may decide not to use.

LEADER'S MATERIALS

To lead Part One of this course, you will need the two videocassettes containing sessions 1-12.

One of the advantages of a video course is that a trained teacher and theologian comes into your classroom each week. Pastor Lew presents Christian doctrine in a way that's both clear and appealing to young people.

Each video presentation is about twenty minutes long. (If at all possible, watch the video presentations at home before viewing them with your class.) We suggest at least another thirty minutes for the review quiz and the discussion of the video. An hour for the entire session would be ideal.

Discussing the video is a crucial part of this course. It gives the students a chance to interact with a knowledgeable leader, to clarify information, to discuss issues, to ask their own questions, and to draw personal applications. You don't need to be a theologian or a professional teacher to lead the discussion, but you do need to be a committed Christian who enjoys young people and who understands what the Bible and the church teach.

This leader's guide will help you through each class session. Each session includes Scripture and Belgic Confession references and a statement of purpose that summarizes the video and gives you general and specific goals for the session.

The Perspective section offers additional biblical, historical, and theological insights into the content of the session. Dr. M. Eugene Osterhaven, a retired professor of systematic theology at Western Theological Seminary, Holland, Michigan, wrote these excellent backgrounds for the original course, and we have retained them for this second edition (Robert DeMoor wrote the Perspectives for [new] sessions 3 and 4). We suggest you read and reflect on this section before getting into the session procedures.

The Procedure section provides step-by-step directions for achieving the session's purpose. In it you will find answers to the review quizzes, a guide to presenting each video (we suggest stopping some videos at various points for discussion), and answers to the questions asked in the student session guides. Suggestions for group work, discussion of case studies, personal application, and other learning activities are included. The Closing section of each session presents a variety of group and personal worship options.

VARIETY

Perhaps you're wondering if twelve (or more) video presentations and discussions will have enough variety to hold the interest of active young people.

As we mentioned earlier, you needn't go through all twenty-four sessions in sequence. Any format gets boring if overworked. And of course some students and some entire groups may simply tune out the video for a variety of reasons. However, our experience with the original edition of *What We Believe* strongly suggests to us that the course not only works—it works well.

Remember that the videos are only about twenty minutes long, feature a gifted communicator, and are directed especially to young people. Following the video, your own discussion time can be lively and varied. Notice too that the questions go beyond facts. Case studies, group work, and a variety of opportunities for personal application should help hold the group's interest. And we've included many creative options that take you beyond the basic questions in the session guide.

As a leader you can use your own creative approaches to inject still more variety into the sessions, if needed. Here are a few ideas:

- Turn off the video and give your own lecture to the group or help the students discover the main idea directly from Scripture and the Belgic Confession.
- Have students compete in teams on the review quiz and the Bible Trivia. Use small groups to work on the questions.
- Ask a pair of students to lead the class discussion for a session.
- Appoint pairs of students to design the concluding worship activities.
- Invite a guest speaker into your classroom.
- Take a field trip to a neighboring church that's markedly different from your own congregation.

HOME CLASSROOMS

If it's practical, try meeting with your students in your home. Young people are more likely to be relaxed and open when gathered around a television set in your family room than seated in rows of folding chairs in church. You can ask students to take turns bringing refreshments.

Teaching in your home does cut down class size to perhaps a dozen or less, but a small group is great for interacting and really getting to know each other.

EVALUATION

We welcome your comments on this course. Please contact us at 1-800-333-8300 or e-mail us at editors@crc publications.org. Thank you.

CRC Publications Staff

Revelation and Religion

SCRIPTURE

Psalm 8; Psalm 19:1-4; Romans 1:19-20

BELGIC CONFESSION

Article 2

PURPOSE

In his first video presentation of *What We Believe,* Part One, Pastor Lew introduces himself and the course, then explains the circumstances that motivated Guido de Brès to write the Belgic Confession. After giving today's Bible Trivia questions, Pastor Lew defines revelation and religion. General revelation, he says, has three parts: nature, history, and conscience. The video concludes with the answers to the Bible trivia questions.

After today's session, students should be more aware of how God reveals himself to them personally through general revelation. They should be able to name the author of the Belgic Confession and explain the context in which it was written. They should be able to define *revelation, religion,* and *general revelation,* giving an example of what they personally have learned about God through nature, history, and conscience.

PERSPECTIVE

This session begins a two-part, twenty-four–session study of Reformed doctrine, or—as it is more commonly called in the churches—catechism. Instead of the experience-based, sin-salvation-service order of doctrines that we find in the Heidelberg Catechism, this course follows the more intellectual order of the Belgic Confession. We begin, therefore, not with "What is your only comfort?" but with "The means by which we know God" (the caption of Article 2).

As Pastor Lew points out in the video, there are two such means: creation and the Bible. These are often referred to as general and special revelation. General revelation includes nature, history, and conscience; special revelation is God's self-disclosure to Israel under the old covenant and to the early church under the new form and meaning of the covenant in Jesus Christ. This week's session concentrates on general revelation and the phenomenon of religion that results from it.

In contrast to the common idea—one with which your students would probably agree—that some people are religious while others are not, this session teaches that all people are religious by nature. As Calvin says, if people do not know the true God, rather than having no god at all, they will make one for themselves. This common religiousness is, from a Reformed perspective, a very important teaching that surfaces again in our ideas of sin, human responsibility, and faith.

Why are all people religious? Because God manifests himself to everyone "daily in the formation of every part of the world, and daily presents himself to public view in such a way that men cannot open their eyes without having to behold him" (John Calvin, *Institutes,* 1, 5, 1). To Calvin, the universe is a gigantic mirror in which we see God. Before reminding his readers that it is dangerous to confuse God with his works, he even suggests that a pious soul could call nature God (*Institutes,* 1, 5, 5). As the psalmist says, "The heavens declare the glory of God" (Ps. 19:1).

Besides the voice of creation, there is also the voice of our conscience. One chapter of Calvin's *Institutes* is entitled "The Human Mind Naturally Endued with the Knowledge of God." Rather than a small, sharp voice that warns us when we err, our conscience should be understood as an inner knowledge or awareness of God, blurred by sin, that witnesses to us of God (Acts 14:17; Rom. 7:22) and leaves us "without excuse" (Rom. 1:20). Because God continues to be in dynamic rapport with his creation (and with us, God's creatures) and because God gives us the capacity to receive his message, none of us can plead innocence, for we all witness something of God's glory.

How history reveals God may be harder to explain to your students. They may think of history as an objective record without any moral element. You might raise the question of whether, looking back, we can see something of God's judgment in, say, the downfall of Nazi Germany or the collapse of Communism in the former Soviet Union. The Scripture is as certain about God's judgment in history as it is about God's mercy. In both, God reveals himself to all people.

The danger of this teaching of general revelation teaching is that it may lead to an independent natural theology. The First Vatican Council (1870) declared (and the 1950 encyclical "Of Mankind" restated) that God "may be certainly known by the natural light of human reason" as creator, one and true, the Lord, and the fount of true morality; it added that the natural mind can obtain "a very fruitful idea" of the mysteries revealed by special revelation. Some post-Reformation Protestants have followed Rome in such an unbiblical adulation of natural theology.

John Calvin makes a helpful distinction between general revelation and our ability to appreciate it: "The demonstration of God, whereby he makes his glory apparent in his creatures, is clear enough with respect to its own brightness; but with respect to our blindness, it is not sufficient" (Commentary on Rom. 1:20). Human beings are incurably religious, but they are also incurably rebellious.

In his heavy criticism of natural theology, Karl Barth even tossed out general revelation, insisting that Jesus Christ, as witnessed to in the Bible, is the only source of our knowledge of God. Barth rejected the older Reformed view that through general revelation all people are religious, that is, they sense the reality of God and know God's moral judgments. Today, however, the one-sidedness of Barth's position is again clear. Scripture and the confession both teach us: Natural theology? No! General revelation? Yes!

Looking forward to the next session, recognize that Article 2 of the Belgic Confession, in presenting general and special revelation as parallel sources of our knowledge of God, leaves an unanswered question: Are these two sources independent of each other? How are they interrelated? In the phrases "to us" and "before our eyes," the confession points to an answer. The Bible speaks to us, believers, as we stand in nature, conscience, and general history. And natural revelation is seen by eyes that have been enlightened by special revelation. These two sources are not side-by-side but interdependent.

PROCEDURE

Video Presentation

To get things started on a friendly note, provide some cookies and pop or other refreshments for your students to enjoy. That way you can chat with them as they arrive and they'll have something to do before class begins.

You really don't need to say much by way of introducing this course, since Pastor Lew does that on today's video. Do explain, though, that the videos are only part of each session (about twenty minutes)—talking about the video and the ideas it sparks is really the most important part of the course. And let the students catch something of your own enthusiasm about reviewing the basics of what we believe. There is important content to cover, but we will have fun along the way!

Hand out the first session guide and pens. Ask everyone to watch for the definitions of the words (highlighted in captions on the video) listed at question 1 under the heading "Video Discussion Guide." Students can jot these down as they have time. (We'll be going over these definitions later, so it doesn't matter if students get everything down word-for-word.)

Show the video nonstop. Ask everyone to write Bible Trivia answers in their session guides (Pastor Lew gives answers to these at the end of the video).

Video Discussion Guide

Use this section of the session guide to help you discuss the video, raise related issues, and apply the session. Encourage students to jot answers and notes on their session guides.

Here are the questions (repeated in **bold** from the session guide) and suggested answers:

1. **Briefly define the following terms:**

   a. **Belgic Confession:** A confession of faith written by Guido de Brès in 1561. It is called the *Belgic* Confession because it was written in what we today call Belgium. It was written to prove to those persecuting the church that those of the Reformed faith professed the truth of Scripture.

   b. **revelation:** God showing or displaying himself to humanity. God communicates knowledge of himself to us so that we may know him, love him, worship him, and serve him (Louis Berkhof, *Manual of Christian Doctrine*).

TIP

This is not a course on the Belgic Confession, but we will be referring to specific articles from the confession during most sessions. While the video does display quoted sections from the confession, you may also want to provide your students with copies of this historic confession (see the back of the *Psalter Hymnal* or order individual copies of the Belgic from CRC Publications). If the Belgic Confession is not one of the standards of your church, you can choose not to discuss it during your sessions. If you are going to use the Belgic, you might read its introduction.

c. **religion:** our response to God's revelation. Note that true religion is receiving a correct revelation from God and then responding properly to that revelation.

d. **general revelation:** God showing or displaying himself in a nonredemptive (nonsaving) way to all people through nature, history, and conscience.

OPTION

Ask the group if their own religious background and training placed a greater emphasis on facts ("head") or on feelings/commitment ("heart"). Which of the two emphases do they think is most needed in the church today?

2. **Why is knowing the basic facts about what we believe just as important as having the right feelings or commitment?**

As Pastor Lew says, if we don't have the right facts, facts drawn from the Bible, then we don't have the basis for making a commitment, and we will be unable to explain our commitment to others in a way that makes sense to them.

3. **General revelation in nature: You are outdoors in the mountains, looking at a sky full of brilliant stars. Or you are taking a hike through an autumn forest. Or you are watching a thunderstorm roar in over a lake. Think about a personal encounter with God's world that impressed you. What did it show you about God?**

Ask for volunteers to give examples of an encounter with God's world that impressed them with God's greatness and goodness, God's sense of order and detail, God's majesty and beauty, creative power, provision, and so on. Note how Article 2 of the Belgic Confession says that the universe is "like a beautiful book in which all creatures, great and small, are as letters to make us ponder the invisible things of God: his eternal power and his divinity." You may want the class to read from Psalm 19:1-4 or Psalm 8, either now or at the close of the session.

4. **General revelation in history. Think of a recent event in your nation's history or your personal history. What did that event show you about God?**

TIP

You'll want to caution your young people that we are not always able to understand just what God is teaching us by world events or by events in our own lives. Sometimes it takes years before God's intentions are clear. Sometimes we never find out for sure.

Certainly God teaches us lessons about himself and our relationship to him through our corporate and individual history. For example, think of the April 20, 1999, massacre of thirteen teens at Columbine High by two student gunmen who ended their rampage by shooting themselves. Witnesses said one of the gunmen put a shotgun to Cassie Bernall's head and asked if she believed in God. When she said yes, he shot her. Cassie's death—and those of the other twelve victims—shook teens and adults all over the world. Josh, the young man who overheard Cassie's exchange with the gunman, later said, "Until that day, I just took everything for granted. I guess I looked at being a teenager as being immortal. Now I realize you can leave this earth at any given point in your life" (Misty Bernall, *She said Yes: The Unlikely Martyrdom of Cassie Bernall,* Plough Publishing House, 1999, pp. 134-135).

5. **General revelation in conscience: Suppose you hurt someone at school by insulting her in front of her friends. That night you can't get to sleep. You begin to regret deeply what you did. How has God used your conscience to reveal himself? What has been revealed?**

   In this case, God spoke through the conscience to create a sense of restlessness and guilt. By so doing, God revealed his desire for mercy and kindness in our lives.

6. **General revelation is nonredemptive, says Pastor Lew. It can't save us. Why not?**

   It's not hard to think of reasons why general revelation alone can't save us, though it can lead us to God by showing us something of his goodness and might. Sin has dulled both general revelation itself and our perception of it. More important, general revelation does not show us Jesus Christ and the way of salvation. Special revelation is needed to save sinners.

7. **Imagine an isolated tribe in the dense tropical rainforests of Brazil. Untouched by civilization, members of this tribe have never heard the gospel. Yet they live by a strict moral code: People who are caught stealing have their hand cut off. Capital punishment is the penalty for murder. The tribe worships the sun, trusting it to provide them with food, prosperity, and long life.**

   Where do you think this tribe got its sense of morality and its sense of the divine? Is this tribe religious?

   Can this tribe give the excuse that it has not been introduced to the one true God? Why or why not? What do Romans 1:19-20 and Article 2 of the Belgic Confession say about this?

   May we say with finality that this tribe is not saved? Why or why not? What implications are suggested for mission work?

   This case study should make for some interesting discussion that can serve as a good summary of the session so far.

   Where did the tribe get its sense of morality and sense of the divine? Mainly from close observation of nature, but perhaps also from the way their basic needs were met, and certainly from that inborn sense of the divine that all people have. The tribe is "religious" because its members have responded to God's general revelation by developing a strict moral code and by worshiping the sun as their deity.

   Can this tribe give the excuse that they have never been introduced to the one true God? Let the class give their opinions. Some students will wonder how the tribe can possibly be held responsible for failing to recognize the one true God from general revelation. Then read Article 2 of the Belgic Confession and Romans 1:19-20. Both speak of humanity being "without excuse" because of general revelation.

OPTION

Ask your class if they think all people are created with a conscience, a sense of right and wrong, good and bad. If so, why don't they behave in right ways toward God? (Because sin has muted or silenced their conscience.) Talk about the extent to which believers should rely on that small "inner voice."

Of course we may not judge who will and who will not be saved in the end. That is up to God to decide. But as we understand the Bible, we believe that the only way to the Father is through Jesus Christ. Our task is to do all we can to bring the good news of Jesus to all people everywhere.

OPTION

If you have time, give students several minutes to write their own version of Psalm 8:1. Then read the prayers for your closing devotion.

Closing

One way to conclude today's session is to read Psalm 8 or Psalm 19:1-4 responsively as a prayer of praise. Or invite students to finish the following prayer starter: O God, you are . . .

Special Revelation

SCRIPTURE

2 Timothy 3:16; 2 Peter 1:20-21

BELGIC CONFESSION

Articles 2, 3, 4, 5, 6, and 7

PURPOSE

The second video presentation reviews general revelation, gives the Bible Trivia questions, then turns to the topic of special revelation. Unlike general revelation, special revelation is redemptive. It includes theophany, voice, miracles, prophets, and Scripture. Pastor Lew explains how books became part of the canon of Scripture. He then defines inspiration and several other terms related to the Bible. The presentation closes with Bible Trivia answers.

After today's session, students should be grateful for God's special revelation found in Scripture. They should be able to distinguish between general and special revelation, describing what's included in general revelation. They should be able to define several key terms that the church uses to describe Scripture, including *canon, authoritative, inspired,* and *infallible.*

PERSPECTIVE

Some years ago the editor of *Fortune* magazine told a group of writers that America's greatest need is for a philosophical absolute. If he were to convert that into the language of the church, he said, it would be "Thus saith the Lord." Today, when nothing seems certain, many long for what is sure. This session deals with the sure word from God we call special revelation.

Because God loves us in spite of our sin, he has given a special revelation of himself and his purposes in addition to the revelation he gives all humanity through creation. Our fall into sin, though scoffed at by many, is a reality that has alienated us from God and brought with it a world of misery. God must react against sin, but instead of letting us perish he has paid the cost of our salvation in the person of his Son, the "Lamb of God" who took away the sin of the world (John 1:29). In a vision the apostle John saw that Lamb standing among other creatures. An angel held a scroll that only the Lamb could take and open, and the assembly worshiped the Lamb and sang:

"You are worthy to take the scroll and to open its seals, for you were slaughtered and by your blood you ransomed for God saints from every tribe and language and people and nation" (Rev. 5:9, NRSV).

Here, in a capsule, is the center of special revelation. It is redemptive, as Pastor Lew says, unlike general revelation, which does not redeem. At its heart is the cross of Christ, by which he made atonement so that we might be restored to our holy God. The Bible is the story of God's redeeming relationship to his people: first the anticipation of salvation in the preparation of a people and then its realization. At a high point in the early history of that story, God disclosed himself to Moses and Israel: "The LORD, the LORD, the compassionate and gracious God, slow to anger, abounding in love and faithfulness, maintaining love to thousands, and forgiving wickedness, rebellion and sin. Yet he does not leave the guilty unpunished" (Ex. 34:6-7).

With increasing fullness God revealed himself to the covenant community. Although God's eyes are too pure to look on evil (Hab. 1:13), his love draws him to us, and he provides what is necessary to reconcile us with himself. Throughout history, God's purpose in creating the world is being realized, a purpose that sin, in all its ugliness, cannot thwart.

God's Word, his special revelation, is not limited to what was written down in the Bible; much was done, said, and written that was not preserved for the church (Luke 11; John 20:30). The Belgic Confession has that in mind when it makes a distinction within special revelation: "holy men of God spoke, being moved by the Holy Spirit," then "afterwards" some of this was put into writing (Article 3). God's original revelation came in a variety of ways, and the part that was written down appears in a variety of literary forms. All of it together constitutes the Word of God. We accept it as such because of Jesus' acceptance of the Old Testament and because of the selection by the early church of the New Testament.

Although there is little problem with the canon of the Old Testament in view of Jesus' attitude, the selection of the canon of the New Testament was more complicated. The church was driven to it by the appearance of other, spurious writings from which it had to distinguish its own precious tradition. That apostolic tradition—that is, the word of the apostles who witnessed Jesus' resurrection—became the norm by which all else was judged, and at its heart were the writings included in our New Testament.

The reason that we receive the Bible as the Word of God is the witness of the Holy Spirit. There are other, subsidiary reasons—the nature of the writings and the testimony of the church—but

> The testimony of the Spirit is superior to all reason. For, as God alone is a sufficient witness to himself in his own Word, so also the Word will never gain credit in the hearts of men until it is confirmed by the internal testimony of the Spirit. It is necessary, therefore, that the same Spirit who spoke by the mouths of the prophets should penetrate into our hearts, to convince us that they faithfully delivered the oracles which were divinely entrusted to them (John Calvin, *Institutes,* 1, 7, 4).

The Belgic Confession teaches in Article 5 that we believe Scripture to be the Word of God because God's own Spirit witnesses in our hearts, not because the church tells us it is so. The ultimate reason that we hold the Bible to be God's Word is God himself, who gives us in it what we need for happiness and salvation (Article 7).

In our smug, complacent age, sin and the need for salvation are sometimes downplayed. Our need for reconciliation with God and his provision for that reconciliation are revealed to us in God's Word—that special revelation God gave us because he loves us.

PROCEDURE

Review Quiz

Distribute today's session guide and pens. Expect some groans and protests when you call attention to the review quiz. Explain that the quizzes are not going to be graded as in school; they are simply a way to help us remember the basics that Pastor Lew tells us about each week. Weekly quizzes will be cumulative, covering information from all previous sessions (from 1-12). Part Two quizzes (sessions 13-24) will not cover material found in Part One.

Give your group a couple of minutes to complete the review quiz. When giving the correct answers, please ask students to correct all false statements:

1. false (Guido de Brès)
2. true
3. true
4. false (to show or display)
5. true
6. false (the third part is conscience, not the Bible)
7. true
8. true
9. true
10. false (religion is our response to God's revelation)

Video Presentation

Explain that today's video is about special revelation. Pastor Lew will have some interesting things to say about the Bible. Ask students to watch for words that describe what we believe about the Bible. Then play today's video.

Video Discussion Guide

Take a moment to ask the students how they did on the Bible Trivia questions. When asked what they liked best about this course, lots of kids said they enjoyed these questions as kind of a fun challenge. That's the function we hope they serve.

Here are some guidelines to today's questions:

1. How does special revelation differ from general revelation?

Special revelation differs from general revelation in that it is redemptive; general revelation is nonredemptive. Special revelation contains all the information we need to have our sins forgiven and be made right with God. While general

> **TIP**
>
> Do what you can to make the review quizzes fun as well as educational. Throw in some of your own silly questions from time to time. Or ask different kids to take turns giving the questions and answers to the class. This may help make the quizzes seem a little less academic to the group.

> **OPTION**
>
> Prior to playing the video, go around the circle, asking each student to contribute one word that describes the Bible (without repeating what someone else said). Make a list of these words on your board.

> **OPTION**
>
> If some students have trouble with the Bible Trivia questions because they don't have much Bible knowledge, consider dividing the class into "trivia teams" of two or three kids each, mixing students with more Bible knowledge with those with less. The teams could even engage in some competition for fun prizes that you bring from time to time. After a few weeks, change the makeup of the teams.

revelation is able to reveal certain characteristics of God, special revelation reveals the way of salvation through Jesus Christ.

2. **List four special ways that God revealed himself during Old Testament times. What's the main way that God's special revelation comes to us today?**

   God revealed himself during Old Testament times in these four special ways:

   a. God's voice: Have students give some examples, as when God spoke from Mount Sinai or to Elijah or at Christ's baptism.

   b. Prophets: Again, have students give a few examples and note that prophets speak for God to the people.

   c. Miracles: Have students give some Old Testament and New Testament examples; then see if they can arrive at a definition of miracles (the video does not supply one). Miracles are generally considered to be supernatural or unusual works of God's providence that have no obvious, natural explanation.

   d. Theophanies: Comes from two Greek words: *Theos,* meaning God; and *phaino,* meaning to show or appear. So *theophany* means a personal appearance or temporary manifestation of God. Theophanies include those times when God himself appeared (for example, to Adam and Eve, to Moses in the burning bush) and those times when an angel representing God appeared (for example, to announce the births of Samson, John the Baptist, and Jesus).

   Ask students how God revealed himself in a very special way in the New Testament (through Christ—see Hebrews 1:1).

   Scripture, of course, is the primary way God's special revelation comes to us today. Call attention to the meaning of the word "Scripture" (writings) and note that this form of special revelation is simply the written record of God's special revelations through theophanies, voice, prophets, miracles, and Christ.

3. **What do we mean when we say a book of the Bible is "canonical?"**

   We mean that it meets the requirements (*canon* means standard or rule) determined by the early Christian church under the guidance of the Holy Spirit. To be part of the Bible, a book had to agree with what the prophets and the apostles said throughout the years. It had to clearly present the message of God. It had to be used and recognized by the church as authentic. And the Holy Spirit had to testify in the hearts of believers that the book came from God.

4. **According to 2 Peter 1:20-21, what was God's role in the writing of Scripture? What was the role of its human authors?**

   God was the source of the content of Scripture, says the *NIV Study Bible* in its comment on these verses. What the Bible says is what God wanted it to say. In a very real sense, Scripture comes "from God." It is, as Pastor Lew said, as if we can open this book and hear God's voice coming from it. It is God's inspired Word.

The role of the human authors of Scripture was more than simply that of recording. They used their own words, tempered by their own experiences and points of view (organic inspiration). They emphasized themes and ideas that were important to the people they were originally writing to (more about that in next week's session). Yet they were guided in all this by the Holy Spirit.

OPTION

The truth of 2 Peter 1:20-21 is reflected in Article 3 of the Belgic Confession (quoted on the video). Take a moment to read that article in unison or have one student read it aloud.

5. **Our church teaches that the Bible is authoritative, inspired, and infallible. What do these words mean? How do they affect the way you read and regard the Bible?**

When we say that the Bible is authoritative, we mean that it is more than just someone's opinion. It's nothing less than almighty God speaking to us! It comes from the highest possible source! And so we need to listen to and obey God's Word.

When we say that the Bible is inspired, we refer to the process by which God "breathed" his Spirit into the Bible writers to guide them to write what he wanted them to write. God moved, influenced, and inspired them by the Holy Spirit. Have students look up 2 Timothy 3:16 and find the word that means "inspired" (God-breathed). Because the Bible is the inspired Word of God, it's set apart from other books. It is unique.

When we say the Bible is infallible, we mean that it is truthful. It can be trusted. It contains all the truth we need to know in order to be saved.

6. **If Bibles were banned and you had absolutely no access to Scripture from this point on in your life, what difference might it make? What, if anything, would you miss? How might your life be changed?**

TIP

When discussing question 6, take care to include yourself in the discussion and avoid using guilt as a motivator to read Scripture. A positive approach works better: What can we gain by spending regular time with God's Word? It's possible that testimonials from some of your students will help more than anything you can say. Be as encouraging as you can.

Encourage your group to be honest with each other. If they feel that the absence of the Bible would make little or no difference in their daily lives, they should feel free to say so. The point is to get some discussion going and, of course, to ask ourselves if God's Word is really as important to us as it could (should) be.

OPTION

Here's an extra question to discuss: Do miracles still happen today? Explain.

Closing

Invite students to share a Bible passage that means something special to them right now. Maybe it's just a verse from a psalm, or maybe it's a story or a parable. Ask for volunteers to read or just tell about their selection.

Close with a prayer of thanks for God's special revelation, the Bible.

OPTION

Psalm 119 (the long one!) has some beautiful passages that describe what God's Word meant to the psalmist, the most familiar being verse 105: "Your Word is a lamp to my feet and a light for my path." Close by reading some of these verses responsively (vv. 10-16, 33-36, 97-105).

God's Word

SCRIPTURE

Luke 15:11-32

BELGIC CONFESSION

Article 7

PURPOSE

Last week we looked at what the church confesses about the Bible—that it is God's authoritative, inspired, and infallible Word. Today's session focuses on the tools and approaches that are helpful when we study the Bible. Pastor Lew briefly describes the role of study Bibles, concordances, commentaries, and Bible dictionaries, then shifts to methods of biblical interpretation. He advises us to avoid moralizing, taking instead an historical-redemptive approach to Scripture. We should also be alert to the context of a passage, to other Scriptures that help us interpret the passage, and to the literal or symbolic nature of the passage.

After today's session, students should be motivated to read and study their Bibles with greater care and insight. They should be able to describe and use at least one of the Bible-study tools listed above. They should be able to define and apply such interpretive terms as *moralism, historical-redemptive approach, context,* and *literal-symbolic.*

PERSPECTIVE

It's all fine and dandy for us to confess that the Bible is God's authoritative, inspired, and infallible Word. But those high-sounding phrases remain empty unless we put them into practice. If we truly believe the things we say about the Bible, then we'll want to devour it. We'll want to make a daily habit of meditating on it and studying it so that we will understand it and learn to do what it says.

It takes sustained effort to read Scripture. As Pastor Lew points out, many passages in the Bible are difficult to understand. Even well-intentioned readers can quickly lose their way. Acts 8 records the story of the Ethiopian official who bounces along in his chariot with a scroll of Isaiah on his lap. He pores over the words in which Isaiah prophecies about the Lamb of God who takes our sins on himself. But he cannot make any sense out of them. It's only by a special act of the Holy Spirit that Philip draws alongside to lead the Ethiopian to a saving knowledge of Jesus Christ.

While God's Word sufficiently reveals all we need to know for our salvation, it takes the Holy Spirit to make that Word live in our hearts. And the means the Spirit so often uses is other believers—fellow Christians who can help us understand and apply what the Bible teaches. Jesus promises as much in John 14:25-26: "All this I have spoken while still with you. But the Counselor, the Holy Spirit, whom the Father will send in my name, will teach you all things and will remind you of everything I have said to you."

It's crucial to realize that the word *you* in this passage is plural. Understanding the Bible is not a matter of our own private feelings, whims, or fancies. The God who gathered us together into one body has also filled us all with one Spirit. No individual has a corner on the truth. Jesus is our one and only Teacher.

Pastor Lew shows us some of the practical implications of that reality. As Christians we should consult and study the Bible *together*—sharing insights, honing our beliefs, honestly and openly engaging in dialogue. Even when we study the Bible on our own we should consult others who have devoted much of their lives to understanding the Bible. Study Bibles, Bible dictionaries, concordances, and commentaries are only some of the tools we can use to enrich our Bible reading with the wisdom of fellow believers. Through that wider input we assure ourselves of fresh insights and of being corrected when our own personal understanding veers away from Scripture's intent.

Pastor Lew mentions a number of important rules that can guide our understanding of Scripture. We'll have a chance to elaborate on them in the lesson. They include reading the Bible in context, interpreting Scripture with Scripture, and determining where the biblical author intends to be taken literally and where the writer speaks metaphorically.

To avoid reducing the Bible to a disconnected series of moral stories, Pastor Lew suggests using what he calls the redemptive-historical approach. This approach, he points out, rightly places Jesus at the center of every passage of Scripture. But what exactly does that mean? We can find an excellent example in Luke 24, where the risen Lord joins two travelers on the road to Emmaus. These two followers of Jesus couldn't put the picture together at all. Jesus, their trusted teacher, has been executed in a horrible way. They had gotten wind of rumors about an empty tomb and angels, and stories that the body of their Master was nowhere to be found.

Without revealing his identity to them, Jesus responds, "'How foolish you are, and how slow of heart to believe all that the prophets have spoken! Did not the Christ have to suffer these things and then enter his glory?' *And beginning with Moses and all the Prophets, he explained to them what was said in all the Scriptures concerning himself*" (vv. 25-27).

Jesus, our Savior and Lord, points out that we can truly find him on every page of the Bible, not just the New Testament but the Old Testament as well. Using a redemptive-historical approach we do not stop at asking the question: How does this story tell me to be a good person? First and foremost we ask: What does this text show me about Jesus Christ and my relationship with him? It helps us to understand that the texts of the Bible do not stand apart from each other; they are intimately connected. What connects them to each other is the love of God fully revealed to us in Jesus Christ, our Savior and Lord. In all our Scripture reading we learn to put him front and center in our lives. And when we do we'll find our Bible reading far more important, interesting, and engaging than any Aesop's fable. Because on the pages of Scripture we actually come face-to-face with our God.

PROCEDURE

Review Quiz

By now your students are probably getting used to starting with a quick review quiz. Here are the answers to today's quiz (again, ask students to correct false statements):

1. false (they are books that meet the requirements for being in the Bible)
2. true
3. true
4. false (the Bible is God's special revelation)
5. false (inspiration refers to the way God "breathed" his Spirit into the Bible writers to tell them what he wanted them to write.
6. false (their own word choice and personalities come through—organic inspiration)
7. true
8. true
9. true
10. false (all people receive God's general revelation)

Video Presentation

Before showing today's video, ask the group this question: If the Bible came with a "help" key similar to what we have on our computers, what would you like it to help you do?

List to any suggestions, then explain that today's session will focus on various "helps" for reading our Bibles. Students may jot down answers to questions 1 and 2 as they watch the video.

OPTION

Before watching the video, ask for volunteers to pantomime some definitely wrong ways to read the Bible. Here are some examples: close eyes, open Bible, then point to verse, read it, repeat the process; read just before dropping off to sleep; read for thirty seconds or less, timing yourself and acting pleased when you're done; stop after every other word to look up a reference in a huge Bible commentary or dictionary. To get things started, you may want to give a sample demonstration for the group.

Video Discussion Guide

Review answers to the first two questions together.

1. Four Bible study tools that Pastor Lew mentions are

- study Bibles
- concordances
- commentaries
- dictionaries

TIP

It would be helpful for you to bring examples of each study tool to show the group.

OPTION

If your church has a computer, chances are the pastor has a concordance software package. Maybe the class could gather in the pastor's study and see how that works, along with some of the other tools the pastor uses to prepare sermons.

TIP

One thing you don't want to do is turn off someone who's into Bible reading but lacks the maturity to avoid moralizing. Such persons could really be stung by too rough a criticism of something they recognize themselves doing. So go easy. Point out the flaw, as Pastor Lew does, but at the same time commend those who read God's Word and attempt to apply it to their lives. Be sure students don't conclude that we shouldn't relate the Bible to our daily living.

Near the end of the video, Pastor Lew also mentions reading a passage in modern English translations as a help in understanding it and making it "come alive."

2. Define and give an example of each of the following:

a. moralism or moralizing:

This is the practice of drawing a lesson for daily living from a passage while ignoring the main meaning or point of the passage. Examples of moralizing cited by Pastor Lew include using the story of the feeding of the five thousand to advocate sharing your lunch; seeing the parable of the Good Samaritan as simply instructing us to help hurting people; and reading the story of Ruth as a moral tale about being nice to your mother-in-law.

b. historical-redemptive approach:

This is a mouthful that probably won't mean a whole lot to your students, even with Pastor Lew's explanation. But it's worth your time to go back and explain in more detail. The Perspective section will help you do just that. The basic idea is that we need to read a passage in the light of what it tells us about God and our salvation. As Pastor Lew points out, this involves asking how the passage gets its meaning through Jesus Christ. Walk back through a couple of examples cited by Pastor Lew, just to be sure the group catches on. In the story of the feeding of the five thousand, we see the power of God in providing for his people, physically and spiritually. Jesus himself becomes "the bread of life." In the story of Ruth, we see God preparing the way for the great kinsman-redeemer, Jesus Christ.

Here's a simple question that we can ask of most passages to get at the historical-redemptive perspective: What does this passage tell us about God and the way that God is working to save his people?

c. reading in context:

Thanks to sound bites and tabloids, your group will know what it means to be quoted out of context. The same principle applies to the Bible—we have to look at what precedes and follows a passage if we are going to understand it correctly. Pastor Lew cites three examples: first, interpreting Christ's invitation in Revelation 3:20 in the context of the church, not individuals. Second, seeing Paul's beautiful chapter on love in the context of what it means to be filled with the Spirit. And third, understanding Genesis 6:4 in the context of the corruption of the times rather than as a bizarre example of marriage between heavenly creatures and humanity.

d. S.I.S.:

Stands for the principle of Scripture interpreting Scripture. Thus we must read the emphasis in Revelation 20:12 (and other passages) on being judged according to our deeds in light of passages such as Ephesians 2:8, which says we are saved by grace through faith. The cry in Ecclesiastes 1—

"everything is meaningless"—needs to balanced with other passages that say life is meaningless only if not rightly related to God.

e. literal vs. symbolic approach:

Some passages, such as Romans 3:23 ("All have sinned") need to be taken literally. They mean exactly what they say. But other passages, such as David's comment that God makes him "lie down in green pastures" should be taken as a symbol or figure of peace and contentment under God's loving care.

3. Practice

We suggest that you use the remainder of the session to give students at least a taste of applying the various methods of Bible study described in the video. We've also included a question that asks students to use a concordance if they have access to one.

> **TIP**
>
> If you can round up several *NIV Study Bibles*, have the students use them for this part of the session. These Bibles include a small concordance and helpful footnotes. If you have other Bible study tools available (Bible dictionaries, commentaries, atlases), you may want to make up some questions that students can answer using these tools.

a. Use a Bible concordance to track down the following:

- **the location of the parable of the rich man and Lazarus** (Luke 16:19-31)
- **a chapter in which Jesus refers to hell three times** (Matthew 5:22, 29, 30)
- **an Old Testament passage about sharing your food with the hungry** (Isaiah 58:7; Ezekiel 18:7; Proverbs 22:9)

b. What morals or "lessons" could you draw from the parable of the lost son while missing its main message? (Luke 15:11-32)

Read the parable at this time; it will be used as the basis for the next two questions. Possible answers include the following: don't run away from home; family will come through in the end; don't waste your time and money in wild living; admit it when you've made a mistake; don't be jealous of other family members.

c. Look at the chapter in which the parable of the lost son is located. What precedes the parable that helps us understand its meaning? What is the context of this parable? How does this help us understand the parable?

The context here is that the Pharisees have been muttering against Jesus for associating with sinners. They think the love of God ought to be limited to the righteous and holy. Jesus tells three parables that contrast this narrow, exclusive view with the broadness and inclusive love of God. The father in the parable of the lost son welcomes the wandering son home. The elder brother complains, just as the Pharisees were complaining that Jesus welcomed sinners. The context helps us understand why Jesus told this parable and gives us some insights into its meaning.

d. What does this parable show us about God and the way that God is working to save his people (historical-redemptive approach)?

If there is a single passage that captures the heart of salvation, this may well be it. Here is a picture of a loving Father who doesn't give up on his wandering children but runs down the road to greet them when they come to their senses and finally head home. It is the good news of the gospel compressed into one unforgettable story in which each of us can see ourselves and the God who loves us.

e. **Are parables like the one about the lost son literal—that is, they mean exactly what they say—or are they symbolic—that is, they suggest meaning beyond what they actually say?**

A parable is a good example of a type of biblical literature that carries meaning beyond the literal story. Sometimes we may miss the nonliteral meaning, as David initially did when Nathan told him about the rich man who stole the sheep from the poor man. But the meaning behind the narrative is always there. You may want to give other examples from Scripture. Some are easy—for example, most of us don't think that the streets of heaven will literally be paved with pure gold (Rev. 21:21); we see that description as a metaphor for the splendor of heaven. Other passages are more difficult. For instance, is hell actually a place of torment and thirst and fire as Jesus describes it in the parable of the rich man and Lazarus? Or was Jesus making quite a different point about people not listening to him? When Revelation 20:6 speaks of a "thousand-year" reign of Christ, does it mean a literal thousand years or is it symbolic language in a symbolic book? A fair number of theological arguments revolve around this issue of literal vs. nonliteral meaning.

OPTION

Assign individual students or small groups to one of the five methods described under question 3. One group could work on moralism, another on context, and so on. Have the groups report to the whole class when they're ready.

4. **What helps you when you read and study the Bible? Maybe something that *you* do will help others. Please share any ideas.**

Here's a chance for your students to refer to their own reading of Scripture. What do they personally find helpful? They may say something as simple as "I try to read a chapter at a time and work my way through a book," or "I try to imagine myself as one of the characters in the story," or "I underline the verse that speaks to me most clearly." Sharing these kinds of ideas can be very affirming—it says that kids are reading the Bible and that they are getting something out of that reading.

Closing

Ask the students to join you in a short meditation on the parable of the lost son. Ask them to close their eyes and to imagine themselves as the lost son or daughter in the parable. Ask them to think of ways that they have wandered from the Father (pause for half a minute or so). Then invite them to see themselves heading down the road toward home, being welcomed by the Father, who throws a great party in their honor (pause again). Close this time by thanking God that we who were once dead are now alive, and that we who were lost are now found.

OPTION

Go around the circle and invite students to offer short prayers of thanks for God's Word. If they wish, they can simply complete this statement: Dear God, thank you that your Word is . . .

Then close with thanks for God's holy Word.

Apologetics

SCRIPTURE

1 Peter 3:15-16

BELGIC CONFESSION

Article 7

PURPOSE

Note: For the remaining video presentations, the video summaries will not mention the Bible Trivia questions and answers; simply assume that the questions and answers will be part of each video.

Today's video begins with "faith questions" from several high school students. Pastor Lew then raises the question of how we can have confidence that our faith is true. In the early days of Christianity, he says, Christians were often persecuted by people who misunderstood Christian beliefs and practices. In response, the church produced *apologists* such as Justin and Augustine who defended the Christian faith. Today, in the Western world at least, Christians may give their testimony and worship God without fear of persecution; in fact, many people in our culture believe that when it comes to God, it's OK to believe just about anything. "Truth" just can't be nailed down in the world of religion as it can be in the world of science. That's faulty thinking, says Pastor Lew, because these same people will uncritically accept, say, the love of their mothers, which certainly can't be proven. Yet they cannot accept the truth about the love of God. The truth about God, while not irrational or unreasonable, ultimately comes down to a matter of the Holy Spirit working in our hearts to convince us that our faith is true.

After today's session, your students should have a renewed confidence that their faith in God is real and defensible. They should be able to describe the role of apologists in the early church, explain the modern "scientific" approach to faith and its weaknesses, and respond to those who ask them to defend their belief in Jesus.

PERSPECTIVE

Is ours a reasonable faith? Does it make sense to be a Christian? Can we explain to others not only what we believe but also why we believe it? Are we good *apologists* for our faith? Pastor Lew tosses these important challenges our way in this session.

The Bible itself is very clear: "Always be prepared to give an answer to everyone who asks you to give the reason for the hope that you have. But do this with gentleness and respect" (1 Peter 3:15).

As we saw from the video, in the early days of the church apologists had to defend the truth of the gospel in the light of those who considered Christianity a threat to civil order. Today we no longer face the threat of that kind of persecution in North America, although in many parts of the globe believers still face the dreadful challenge of defending their faith at the cost of imprisonment and even death.

But that doesn't mean that we don't have to be able to defend our faith in our society as well. Our culture takes scientific fact as gospel truth and considers gospel truth as only a matter of personal opinion. Our society scorns those who would dare suggest that they know *the* Truth, *the* Way, and *the* Life. "Prove it," they say.

Pastor Lew offers two responses to that challenge.

First, while we cannot offer "proof" in the same way that we can prove that ice melts at 32 degrees Fahrenheit, much important evidence corroborates our faith. For example, we can show that the Bible was not written by some weirdo in the last century. We can demonstrate that it was assembled over hundreds of years by people who witnessed amazing events. The parting of the Red Sea and the resurrection of Jesus, to name just two of these events, clearly testify to God's existence, God's love for his people, and the reliability of God's promise of eternal life. Had these historical events not occurred, they would have been disproved at the time they were recorded. (Those who doubted the resurrection of Jesus simply needed to produce his body to show that Easter was a farce.) But that's not what happened. In fact, just the opposite happened. The Israelites became a great nation and the church of Jesus Christ exploded into the world, taking over the hostile Roman world in three short centuries.

Many witnesses have seen with their own eyes what God has done. You find their testimony in the Bible. Did they make it all up? We cannot *prove* or disprove their testimony today. To decide whether they told the truth, we need to read their accounts. Proof? No. If there were such proof, then every nonbeliever would be like those who still claim that the earth is flat. But we have more than enough evidence and more than enough eyewitnesses to demonstrate that ours is not a blind faith but a reasonable one.

Pastor Lew's second point is that we accept *lots* of things that are not provable. In fact, the really *important* things in life are never open to proof. How do we prove our parents love us? How can we scientifically show that there is life after death or that God does or does not exist? We can't. How can science help us find the meaning of life or even tell us why any of us should bother getting through the rest of this day? It can't.

The most important things in our lives—love, hope, joy—don't fit under a microscope. Yet we know they are real. We *know* even though they have not been proven scientifically. Our faith places us on a firm and secure foundation even when the test tubes remain safely locked up in the lab.

Ultimately we know we believe in God because God, through the Holy Spirit, gives us saving faith. That faith is not the product of our own scientific experimentation. It is not the result of our own heroic efforts to talk ourselves into it. We believe because God's Spirit convinces us that the witnesses whose evidence is recorded in Scripture spoke the truth. And when we read their words that same Spirit allows us to encounter our risen Lord. Jesus promised, "I will not leave you as orphans; I will come to you. Before long, the world will not see me anymore, but you will see me" (John 14:18-19). Maybe we can't *prove* it. But we cannot doubt what we ourselves experience over and over again—that daily encounter with our risen Savior and living Lord.

PROCEDURE

Review Quiz

Here are suggested answers to this week's fill-in-the-blank quiz (allow for some variations):

1. the Bible
2. inspired or inspiration
3. Bible dictionary, concordance, study Bible, commentary
4. moralizing or moralism
5. context
6. God or Jesus
7. interpreting
8. literal
9. nature
10. the Belgic Confession

Video Presentation

To introduce today's video about apologetics, hold up a Bible and ask the group to think about how they would respond to someone who attacked the Bible and their beliefs by saying something like this:

> When I think about your faith and how it all rests on this one book, I've got to wonder. For one thing, every world religion has its own Bible, right? So how do you know your Bible is right and the others are wrong? And then there's all kinds of stuff in this Bible of yours that just doesn't add up. Do you really believe that because Eve listened to a talking snake the whole world fell into sin and you were born a sinner? And do you really believe that God came down to earth and died for your sins, arose from the dead and went back to heaven, where you plan on seeing him someday? I ask you, what's logical

about this? Now, it's perfectly fine for you to believe this. But don't ask me to, because you really can't prove any of it.

Invite reactions, and then explain that today's video talks about this very important issue under the funny-sounding title of "apologetics," that is, defending what we believe (not saying "I'm sorry" about it but arguing for it, telling others why we believe).

OPTION

Before class arrange to stage a dialogue with a student from your group. Have the dialogue focus on the issue described above, with one person representing the Christian point of view and the other person attacking that point of view. You may want to rehearse once before your presentation to the class.

Video Discussion Guide

1. What were some of the things that Christians living in the first few centuries were accused of? What role did the "apologists" play?

Among other things, early Christians were accused of disloyalty to the Roman Empire because they worshiped God alone, not the emperor, who claimed to be worthy of worship because he was descended from the gods. In addition, their communion services, called "love feasts," were misrepresented as wild, drunken parties and the sacrament of the Lord's Supper was misunderstood as cannibalism. Church leaders including Justin and Augustine defended Christians against these and other false charges. They became known as apologists, people who defended the Christian faith against attacks by its enemies.

OPTION

Distribute a notecard to students and ask them to list what they consider to be the top three enemies of the church today (either external or internal). Then go around the circle and ask students to read their lists. Have another student keep track of the three most frequently mentioned responses.

2. What's meant by "the scientific method"? What happens when this method is applied to God?

The scientific method, so prevalent in Western culture, relies on external proof or evidence to determine whether or not something is true. A hypothesis is stated and then extensively tested. If the data collected consistently proves the hypothesis, then the hypothesis becomes a principle or law. If something cannot be proven in this way, it's not regarded as true.

This method cannot be used to prove that God exists and that all things that happened in the Bible are true. The conclusion of those who apply this method to religion boils down to this: While it's fine for you to believe anything you wish about God, there is no hard, scientific evidence for your belief. You cannot prove that what you believe is true.

3. How would you defend your faith against the accusation that because it cannot be conclusively "proven" to be true, it is therefore irrational and illogical?

Give the students time to think this through, then summarize their responses on your board or on newsprint. Students may recall what Pastor Lew said about the evidence for the existence of God in the need for a "first cause," in the intricate order and design of the natural world, in the way modern archeology supports biblical facts, in the way the Bible and the church have stood the test of time. Remind them of the evidence that our faith is real and is based on historical fact. Invite students to add their own reasons as well.

OPTION

Have students work in pairs or groups of three to develop a response to this question, outlining their ideas on a sheet of newsprint. Then review their responses with the whole group.

4. **Are one person's beliefs about God just as valid as another person's beliefs? Why or why not?**

   As Pastor Lew points out, this approach often stems from a belief that since nothing about God or God's revelation can be proven, it really doesn't matter what a person believes. As Christians, we accept as truth what God tells us in Scripture and what the Spirit of God affirms in our hearts.

5. **What point was pastor Lew trying to make with his story of the young person standing by his mother's casket and being asked if she loved him?**

   His point is a crucial one: that "truth" can be determined in ways other than supplying logical or philosophical proof, that what we know to be true in our hearts is an equally valid way to determine truth. It's ironic that persons who are perfectly willing to defend, say, the unprovable fact that their mother loved them are unwilling to accept the facts of God's existence and the truth of Scripture.

6. **"Always be prepared to give an answer to everyone who asks you to give the reason for the hope that you have. But do this with gentleness and respect . . ." (1 Peter 3:15-16).**

   - **In what situations, present or future, might you see yourself possibly being asked why you are a Christian or why you believe in God?**
   - **Suppose one of your good friends doesn't believe in Jesus. One day your friend asks you, flat-out, why you believe in Jesus. What would you say?**

   In response to the first question, students might mention such situations as being with friends who have some doubts about their own faith and want to know why you believe. Or perhaps an encounter with nonbelievers or persons from other religions at work, at school, in a chat room on the Internet . . . the possibilities are many. Someday we may well be surprised to hear someone ask us this very question.

   Give students time to jot down their own response on the second part of the question. This needn't be a long or complete statement. You may want to remind them of what Pastor Lew said: "I know that I have the truth in my heart because the Holy Spirit tells me." After giving students time to write, invite them to share their responses with the class. This may be easy for some students, very difficult for others. Even if only one or two group members share their statements, this can be a beautiful time of encouragement and affirmation for the class. But be sure to make participation voluntary.

TIP

Some of your students may not be ready to say why they believe in Jesus simply because they haven't arrived at that point in their faith journey. You will want to acknowledge this at the start and invite students to be honest about where they are spiritually. Many adolescents are going through a time of searching for faith, of not knowing exactly what they believe. They may be questioning the faith taught them by their parents and the church. They need to hear that this is often a part of the process of coming to a true and lasting faith.

OPTION

Once students have had time to write out a response to the second question, ask them to role-play their answers with one other person in the group. One person can role-play the believer, the other the person asking the question.

If you've not referred to the Cassie Bernall story (session 1), you may want to do so at this time. Asked at gunpoint if she believed in God, this courageous young person said yes and died for her convictions.

Closing

A confession of faith that began with the early church and is still recited throughout Christendom today is the Apostles' Creed. Recite it (or read it from your church's hymnal) in unison with your group. As leader, close by giving thanks for the faith of your students, and ask God to nurture their faith and yours.

OPTION

Instead of the Apostles' Creed, read Revelation 4:11 in unison to close today's session.

The Attributes of God

SCRIPTURE

Psalm 103 or 139

BELGIC CONFESSION

Article 1

PURPOSE

Today's video presentation defines attributes as qualities or characteristics of someone or something. Pastor Lew uses the example of marriage to talk about the importance of knowing one's own attributes and the attributes of a partner. Citing Article 1 of the Belgic Confession, he describes the incommunicable attributes of God as those qualities only God possesses (almighty, infinite, eternal, and so on). This raises an interesting question: Can God create a rock so big that he can't lift it? (The answer is no, because God is bound by his "Godness"—by who he is). Knowing God's power and might is helpful and comforting in our dangerous world, says Pastor Lew. He then describes God's communicable aspects, those qualities God shares with us (justice, love, truth, knowledge, creativity, and so on).

Knowing how we are like God helps us "connect" with God and live in a better relationship with him.

After today's session, students should have a better understanding of and appreciation for how God is at once like us (communicable attributes) and totally unlike us (incommunicable attributes). They should be able to define attributes, list several of God's communicable and incommunicable attributes, and explain what good it does to know these things about God.

PERSPECTIVE

What is God like? That's the subject of this lesson. It has to do with the infinite, incomprehensible Creator and the mystery of his being.

"To whom, then, will you compare God? What image will you compare him to?" (Isa. 40:18).

No one but God himself can describe the living God to us. God's self-disclosure to Israel distinguished Israel's religion from all others. The Gentiles wandered in darkness; Israel had the light of life. Others fashioned gods according to their own fancies; the God of Abraham could not be contained in the highest heaven (2 Chron. 6:18). The church built on that foundation, believing that God's self-revelation under the Old Covenant—his names, attributes, and purpose—was confirmed and amplified with the coming of Christ. Then God's perfection took on a deeper meaning and his tri-personal nature was revealed.

In one sense, because God is God, we can never know him as he is; in another sense, we know him because he condescends to dwell in the midst of his people. The Bible says that no one can see God and live (Ex. 33:20); yet God spoke to Moses "face to face, as a man speaks with his friend" (v. 11). Israel wanted God to "bow the heavens and come down"; when he did so in Christ, it was hidden from the wise and revealed to little children (Matt. 11:25). The mystery of a holy God who desires communion with his creatures is as fundamental to our faith today as it was to the Israelites.

Besides holiness and love, the Bible speaks of God's other attributes. God's power, demonstrated in the history of Israel and in the "signs and wonders" and resurrection of Christ, is mentioned frequently (see, for example, Eph. 1:19). So are God's wisdom (Eph. 3:10; Col. 2:3; 1 Cor. 1:21), justice (Rom. 3:21-26), will (Eph. 1:5-11), truth (2 Cor. 1:20), omniscience (Isa. 40), and the rest. This session suggests you ask your class to name other attributes mentioned in the Bible. When the biblical givens are assembled, the attributes can be classified as communicable and incommunicable, as the video says clearly. The first group—the attributes God shares with us—can be divided into (1) those that designate God as Spirit or life: spirituality and invisibility; (2) those that describe him as perfect in his self-consciousness: omniscience, wisdom, and truth; (3) those that point to his ethical nature: goodness, justice, or righteousness, and holiness; (4) regal attributes: will, freedom, and omnipotence; (5) those that summarize the perfection of God: blessedness and glory.

Certain attributes belong to God alone; they cannot be communicated to creatures. These are (1) self-sufficiency or independence; (2) immutability; (3) infinity, including eternity and omnipresence; and (4) oneness, including both number and simplicity.

Thinking about what God is like is both difficult and simple. Thinking about God as love is easy; we understand that. But what does his infinity or simplicity mean to your class? As Pastor Lew says, God is God. And the attributes God has revealed in his Word, the Bible, help us to appreciate him—they inspire our love and praise and worship.

PROCEDURE

Review Quiz

Answers to today's true/false quiz (ask students to orally correct false statements):

1. true
2. true
3. false (Augustine was an apologist for the Christian faith)
4. false (ultimately, we have to accept the existence of God and the truth of the Bible by faith)

5. true
6. true
7. false (the statement describes general revelation)
8. true
9. true
10. false (certain types of writing in the Bible should be read as symbolic, not as literal)

Video Presentation

Hand out the session guides and pens. Ask students to jot down definitions for the words listed in question 1 of the video discussion guide.

OPTION

Stop the video just after Pastor Lew asks if God can create a rock so large he can't lift it. (Be sure to preview the video so you know where this point is—be careful, because the answer immediately follows!) Poll your class to see how many would answer yes and how many no. Talk a little about the reasons for their answers. Then continue the video through to the end.

Video Discussion Guide

1. Definitions

- **attributes:** qualities or characteristics of someone or something
- **God's incommunicable attributes:** qualities only God possesses
- **God's communicable attributes:** qualities we share with God. Please point out that while we "share" these attributes with God, God possesses them in far greater degree than we do.

2. Make a list of the communicable and incommunicable attributes of God. You may want to refer to Article 1 of the Belgic Confession.

Use your board or newsprint to record the list. Invite students to refer to Article 1 of the Belgic Confession for attributes to classify. A sample list follows:

Communicable	Incommunicable
just	eternal
good	almighty
great	infinite
faithful	unchanging (immutable)
loving	beyond understanding (incomprehensible)
merciful	all-knowing (omniscient)
gracious	invisible
wise	present everywhere (omnipresent)
kind	oneness
sovereign	independent
righteous	

TIP

Don't expect most students to use the big words we've included in parentheses on our list; in fact, encourage them to use their own words. You can add the official language later if you wish.

OPTION

Have students divide into groups of two or three and make their lists of attributes on large sheets of paper, using markers. Tape the lists to your wall and draw up a master list.

Have the small groups mentioned above use Psalm 103 as a source of descriptive words for God. The psalm is rich in words that describe God: forgiving, healing, compassionate, giving, righteous, just, gracious, slow to anger, loving, kingly, ruling, and more.

OPTION

During times of extreme crisis, people often feel the presence of God in remarkable ways. Somehow, God's grace gets them through horrible violence, prolonged illness, accident, and loss. Look for fresh examples of this and bring in an article or book from which you can read an excerpt.

3. **How could knowing about God's incommunicable attributes help us? When, for example, might knowing that God is powerful and almighty be especially important to us?**

   You may want to refer to Pastor Lew's comment that he doesn't want a wimpy God. In a dangerous world of violence and unexpected happenings, we need a God who is powerful to act and to save. We need an *almighty* God!

   You should also point out that realizing how great and awesome God is leads to something absolutely essential for every Christian: worship and praise of our great God.

4. **How could knowing that we share certain attributes with God be helpful to us?**

   As Pastor Lew points out, knowing that we are like God in some ways can help us feel closer to God. It can also inspire us to attempt to be more like God in our attitudes and behavior.

5. **Although God reveals himself to us, we need to realize that God is also awesomely mysterious. As finite human beings, we cannot fully know who God is. Give some examples of times when you sense God's greatness and mysteriousness.**

   We ask this question to avoid giving the impression that our list of attributes neatly pins down who God is. Before students give examples of times when they encounter God's greatness and mysteriousness, you may want to read these comments by Cornelius Plantinga from *A Sure Thing:*

   > We get the feeling of awesomeness about God only at certain times and in certain places. If we are alone at night and hear the wind come mysteriously through the trees, we may think of God. If we attend the funeral of someone we love, we may feel the strangeness of death and the mystery of God. Or suppose we step into a large Roman Catholic church. We see statues and smell candles. We sense an atmosphere that is strange and awesome to us. We may feel surrounded by the secret things of God.
   >
   > A mystery is something puzzling, secret, or unknown to us. We read mystery books, watch mystery movies, and observe mysterious persons.
   >
   > Multiply this a thousand times in thinking of the mystery of God. Even when we love God and trust that God loves us, we still cannot see him or know everything about him. . . .

TIP

Your students need to see that you are also deeply impressed with the greatness and mysteriousness of God. Come prepared to tell them of times when you experienced these feelings.

Closing

Invite your group to respond to God's greatness and love in the words of one of the psalms. Psalm 103, read responsively, is a wonderful way to praise God for many of his attributes. Psalm 139 is another excellent choice.

After the reading, invite students to offer sentence prayers praising God for who he is and what he has done for them.

TIP

It may help to give students a simple phrase to complete for their prayer: Dear God, I worship you and praise you for . . .

The Trinity

SCRIPTURE

Deuteronomy 6:4; Isaiah 61:1; Matthew 28:19; Luke 1:35, 3:21-22; 4:18; 2 Corinthians 13:14

BELGIC CONFESSION

Articles 8 and 9

PURPOSE

The sixth video presentation introduces the topic of the Trinity with an example of someone being challenged by Jehovah's Witnesses to prove the Trinity from the Bible. Although the word *Trinity* is not found in Scripture, the three persons of the Trinity are, sometimes in the same passage. The basic issue is whether all three persons of the Trinity are truly God. The church throughout the ages has confessed in its Scripture-based creeds that they are. Father, Son, and Holy Spirit are three distinct persons, yet each is of one essence, fully and completely God. This doctrine of the Trinity distinguishes a true church from many cults. It also enables us to believe that Jesus is our Savior and that God lives in us through the Holy Spirit.

After today's session, your students should have a greater understanding and appreciation of the doctrine of the Trinity. They should be able to define *Trinity,* defend their belief in it using Scripture, and state its importance for their faith.

PERSPECTIVE

Although Israel had a rich conception of God, it was enlarged with the coming of Christ and the gift of the Holy Spirit. It is surprising that the first disciples were convinced that their Lord was God in human flesh—after all, they were pious, monotheistic Jews for whom polytheism was the ultimate sin. To set anyone or anything alongside Yahweh was blasphemy. Yet they did just that with Jesus Christ and the Holy Spirit. Since then the church has believed that the Son and the Spirit are together with the Father, in communion with him from eternity; these three, it confesses, are one God. This doctrine of the Trinity radically distinguishes Christianity not only from the Jehovah's Witnesses, but also from Judaism, Islam, and other religions.

To be sure, the *doctrine* of the Trinity is not laid out as such in the New Testament. However, the New Testament does record the conviction in the hearts of the people that gave rise to this doctrine. On the basis of that record the early church, challenged by alternative beliefs about God that it believed were wrong, worked out the doctrine of the Trinity.

Among those alternative beliefs were two forms of Unitarianism or Monarchianism, as the movement was called. One held that Son and Spirit are not persons but qualities of God. The person of Jesus Christ is not eternal, it said, but bound in time. The titles "Lord" and "God" were given him out of courtesy. God is not tri-personal but one person. The other school said that the three persons are simply different "modes" or manifestations of the one person of God. Their "trinity" was a successive one, rather than one in which the three persons exist at the same time. That these ideas gave the church problems is obvious, and it had to deal with them.

As your class discusses the Trinity, they may come up with ideas similar to the historical positions mentioned above. One useful approach is to have them figure out the logical consequences of either of these positions. For example, if the Son of God did not exist from eternity, could he be God? Can godhead be conferred? Concerning "modalism," in which the persons do not exist simultaneously, to whom did Jesus cry out on the cross? To whom did he pray? Offer atonement?

The belief that there are three persons in one God is confirmed by Scripture. In it Christ is set forth as God as well as man. He is the unique Son of the Father. No one knows him "except the Father, and no one knows the Father except the Son and those to whom the Son chooses to reveal him" (Matt. 11:27). As the Father raises the dead and gives them life, so does the Son. The Father "has entrusted all judgment to the Son, that all may honor the Son just as they honor the Father. He who does not honor the Son does not honor the Father, who sent him (John 5:22-23). Because Jesus called himself God and said that God was his Father, "making himself equal with God" (John 5:18; 10:15), some sought to kill him.

Jesus possesses the attributes and does the work of God, according to the testimony of the New Testament. He raises the dead, judges the world, is said to be the creator and upholder of all things, and receives the honor and worship properly due to God alone. In some places his name is associated with God as equal to him (Matt. 28:19; Acts 2:38; Rom. 6:3; 1 Cor. 1:3; 12:4-6; 2 Cor. 2:14; John 5:23; 14:1). Christ is called God in Scripture (John 1:1; 20:28; Rom. 9:5; Heb. 1:8), and Old Testament descriptions of God are given to Jesus.

The most important of these descriptions is *Lord,* the name for the covenant God of Israel. While there are a few instances in the New Testament where the expression means only "master" or "sir," when the disciples called Jesus their Lord after the resurrection they meant his deity. A comparison of Matthew 3:3 with Isaiah 40:3 or Philippians 2:6-11 with Isaiah 45:20-25 demonstrates this. In both Isaiah passages the Lord God of Israel is the subject. In the New Testament it is "at the name of Jesus" that "every knee should bow . . . and every tongue confess that Jesus Christ is Lord." *Lord* here means God; to the Hebrew mind only God could do what Jesus did. Jesus is seen as Lord—that is, as God as well as man—by the Holy Spirit (1 Cor. 12:3). Thomas's salutation to the risen Christ was "My Lord and my God" (John 20:28).

The Holy Spirit too is presented as a divine person in the New Testament. He is the source of guidance (John 16:13; Acts 8:29, 39; 13:4; 15:28; 16:7); renewal (Tit. 3:5); life (John 3:5-8; Luke 1:35); power (Acts 1:8); comfort (Acts 9:31); joy (1 Thess. 1:6); faith (1 Cor. 12:9); hope (Rom. 15:13); love (1 John 4:7, 13); and a wide variety of gifts (Rom. 12:6ff.; 1 Cor. 12:14), including Scripture (1 Cor. 2:13; 1 Pet. 1:11ff.). The Spirit prays for the saints (Rom. 8:16, 26) and can be sinned against. He is mentioned with the Father and the Son in the baptismal formula and in a benediction. For good reason, then, the early church regarded the Spirit as God along with the Father and the Son. In confessing a trinitarian faith, the church believed that it was fulfilling a pious duty, honoring each of the three persons as God.

Your students may wonder just how important this doctrine is for their faith. Is an understanding of the Trinity necessary for salvation? What is necessary? An acceptance of Christ as the all-sufficient Savior. He is all-sufficient because he came from the Father, became one of us, and did what only God can do. And by his Spirit he lives with us today.

PROCEDURE

Review Quiz

Here are suggested answers to this week's fill-in-the-blank quiz (be sure to allow for variations):

1. qualities, characteristics, descriptions
2. God alone possesses
3. God and people share

4-5. eternal; almighty; infinite; unchanging; incomprehensible; omniscient; invisible; omnipresent; independent; and so on.

6-7. just; good; great; faithful; loving; merciful; gracious; wise; kind; sovereign; righteous; and so on.

8. faith
9. general revelation
10. mysterious

Video Presentation

Before playing this week's video, distribute the session guides and read the case study from today's session guide (Video Discussion Guide, question 1):

> **It's about 4 o'clock, and you just got home from school. An unfamiliar car drives up to your house, and two men get out and knock on your door. You're the only one home. You answer the door and discover that they are Jehovah's Witnesses. They begin to question your beliefs about God. You claim to believe in the Trinity, but they challenge you to prove it from the Bible.**

OPTION

Give each group a large sheet of paper and a marker; have them jot down their answers and then report to the larger group.

How would you respond? What Scripture passages would you direct them to?

After reading the above, distribute Bibles and divide the class into groups of two to four. Ask each group to answer the two questions above. Doing this will prepare them for Pastor Lew's presentation of this question. Allow no more than five minutes for the groups to talk. Then discuss the question with the entire class, letting the groups contribute answers as much as possible.

Begin by asking if any group found the word *Trinity* in the Bible (nope—not there!) Then see if the groups were able to cite some passages (or at least describe some situations) where all three persons of the Trinity are mentioned. List the group's findings on the board or on newsprint. Do not add to the list at this time, since we'll be revisiting the question after the video is shown. If students aren't able to mention any passages or describe any situations, that's OK—tell them to listen closely to today's video, where Pastor Lew gives his response to this question.

TIP

If your students aren't all that familiar with the Bible, don't do the preliminary exercise described above; instead, just show the video and then discuss the case study with the entire class. Students will then have pastor's Lew's responses to the question as a starting point for the discussion.

After this preliminary discussion, play the entire video.

Video Discussion Guide

1. **It's about 4 o'clock, and you just got home from school. An unfamiliar car drives up to your house, and two men get out and knock on your door You're the only one home. You answer the door and discover that they are Jehovah's Witnesses. They begin to question your beliefs about God. You claim to believe in the Trinity, but they challenge you to prove it from the Bible.**

   How would you respond? What Scripture passages would you direct them to?

   Take time now to complete the list of passages or situations that you began before the video. Many passages could be cited (see the Perspective part of this lesson) but at least include the following (ask students to read the verses aloud):

   - Matthew 28:19 (the Great Commission)
   - Luke 1:35 (the angel's visit to Mary)
   - Luke 3:21-22 (Christ's baptism)
   - Luke 4:18 and Isaiah 61:1 (Christ's announcement in the synagogue)
   - 2 Corinthians 13:14 (the benediction)

   Conclude by asking if anyone knows a passage that says God is one God. Read Deuteronomy 6:4 with the class.

2. **Most people agree that the Bible presents three persons: Father, Son, and Holy Spirit. What, then, is the real issue?**

   The existence of three persons is obvious from the passages cited earlier in today's session. The real issue is whether all three persons are fully God. Reiterate the church's repeated affirmation of the biblical teaching that all three persons in the Trinity are of the same essence and are truly and fully God.

Perhaps you will also want to say that the Trinity is something of a mystery. These words from Cornelius Plantinga in *A Sure Thing* may be helpful:

> What, then, is the mystery of the Trinity? There are two things it is not. First, it is not the question of how one divine person could somehow appear in three roles or modes. That is a Christian heresy called "modalism." Second, neither is it the pious confusion sometimes adopted by people who suppose that the doctrine of the Trinity is self-contradictory. They suppose that the doctrine says there are three persons in God, but also only one. That (besides being incoherent) is both unbiblical and uncreedal. The real trinitarian mystery is how three biblically revealed persons can be so radically, gloriously, and inconceivably "in" each other as to have perfectly harmonious and interwoven and interpenetrating will, works, word, knowledge, love, and glory.

3. Read Article 8 of the Belgic Confession. Use it to develop a simple definition of the word *Trinity.*

Students should be able to phrase a simple definition of the Trinity along these lines: The Trinity is one God in three distinct persons: Father, Son, and Holy Spirit.

OPTION

Talk about various comparisons that people have used to help them understand the Trinity. Recall the ones the video mentioned: the egg (shell, white, yoke, yet one egg); the clover (three leaves, one plant). Another common metaphor is that of the three forms of water: liquid, steam, ice). Do students agree with Pastor Lew that accepting the Trinity is "more of a faith thing" than a rational, logical thing?

4. The best-known Christian creed in the world is the Apostles' Creed. Show how it is a trinitarian creed. Which member of the Trinity does the Creed devote most space to? Why?

Take a moment to distribute copies of the Apostles' Creed or find it in the back of your hymnal. Talk about how it is organized around members of the Trinity. Notice how it spends the most time on the second person of the Trinity, Jesus Christ. Perhaps this focus is due to the attacks on the identity of Christ at the time the creed was being formed (first five centuries after Christ).

5. What difference does it make to you personally whether or not you believe the doctrine of the Trinity? Does it really matter? Explain.

Although some may see the doctrine of the Trinity as an irrelevant piece of doctrine, it is central to our faith. To believe in the Trinity is to believe that all three persons are equally God. If Jesus is not God, we have no Savior—for only God can save us from our sins. If the Holy Spirit is not God, then God doesn't really live in us after all. Without the Trinity, there is no salvation, no God-filled hearts and lives, no eternal life.

OPTION

Have students complete these statements in writing:

- Because God the Father is God, I . . .
- Because Jesus is God, I . . .
- Because the Holy Spirit is God, I . . .

Students can share their statements as part of your closing exercise.

Closing

To conclude the session, we suggest having students pair off and take turns reading the benediction found in 2 Corinthians 13:14 to each other: "May the grace of the Lord Jesus Christ, and the love of God, and the fellowship of the Holy Spirit be with you all." If you prefer, simply read the benediction in unison.

OPTION

Supply students with a copy of the Apostles' Creed and read it in unison (or recite it from memory). Or read the Nicene Creed (mentioned in the video), with half the students reading one line, the other half the next line, and so on.

Election

SCRIPTURE

Matthew 24:22, 24, 31; John 15:16; Romans 8:28-30; Ephesians 1:4-5

BELGIC CONFESSION

Article 16

PURPOSE

In his fifth video presentation, Pastor Lew defines election as God choosing those who will be saved. He then reads Article 16 of the Belgic Confession. The rest of the video is structured around the following six questions: (1) What is God's election? (2) Is election found in the Bible? (3) Is it fair? (4) Does God choose people to go to hell? (5) How do I know if I'm elect? (6) How does TULIP fit in with the doctrine of election? Pastor Lew spends the most time answering the first question. He contrasts the position of churches that teach that people come of their own "free will" to God with those that believe God first chooses people, putting the gift of faith within them, before they decide to come to God.

After today's session, students should have a greater sense of security and peace about their personal salvation. They should be able to answer the six questions listed above and compare the Calvinistic interpretation of election with the "free will" perspective.

PERSPECTIVE

It is widely believed that the doctrine of election is an oddity of Calvinism and the Reformed churches. In fact, Augustine worked out the doctrine in the early church; all the medieval theologians and major Reformers held it; and it is written into the creeds of Episcopalian and Lutheran churches. More importantly, the theme of election runs throughout the Bible, from the call of Abraham in Genesis to the end of the New Testament. The video refers to Ephesians 1; consider also Deuteronomy 7:6-8, one of the most unequivocal assertions of sovereign grace in the Bible. Jesus told his disciples that they did not choose him, but he chose them (John 15:16). In Matthew 24 Jesus mentions "the elect" several times. Peter and Paul often used similar terms and, after a sermon by Paul, Scripture notes that "all who were appointed for eternal life believed" (Acts 13:48).

This teaching is a part of the biblical emphasis on grace. Salvation can only come from God. Because of the fall we are a sinful, lost race; apart from grace we are "without hope and without God in the world" (Eph. 2:12). That hardly needs proof these days. A radical doctrine of sin necessitates a radical doctrine of grace—the Bible and the Reformed faith give us both.

Although God's eternal purpose, sometimes called predestination, is enveloped in mystery and is largely hidden from us, the Bible teaches clearly that election is part of a plan he conceived before the creation of the world (Eph. 1:41ff.). Therefore we dare not neglect it. In the Old Testament we find the sharpest insistence on the reality of the divine purpose (Isa. 46:8-10); the New Testament tells about its fulfillment in many places (Eph. 3:11).

Since the Belgic Confession speaks about both election and reprobation, it is important to note that both are not grounded in God's will "in the same manner." Scripture says repeatedly that God has no pleasure in the death of the wicked but that he wants them to repent (Ezek. 18:23, 32; 33:11; 1 Tim. 2:4; 2 Pet. 3:9). Any construction of the doctrine of election that denies this is unbiblical. The only reason that anyone is rejected by God is sin, and sin does not come from God (Canons of Dort, 1, 5). The Synod of Dort condemned the teaching that election and reprobation are both grounded in God's will.

A one-sided emphasis on predestination emerged in Scotland and the Netherlands in the seventeenth century, in England in the eighteenth, and in America in the twentieth century. This failure to teach "the whole will of God" (Acts 20:27) resulted in a denial of God's love for all humankind, on the one hand, and a failure to emphasize evangelism and human responsibility, on the other. Balance is achieved in speaking where Scripture speaks and being silent where it is silent. Unable or unwilling to do this, some have drawn what they thought were logical conclusions from Scripture and have taken positions contrary to other biblical teaching and hence to the holy will of God.

Forty-two years of teaching have taught me that our knowledge is fragmentary, that mystery is a fact of life, and that logic should be used as an instrument only, not as the master of the system. It might even be necessary to affirm a fact and deny the consequence that we or others would like to draw from it.

Since the subject of election is complicated, it is not wise to make it more so by introducing extreme positions of which students may be unaware. It's also a subject that's bound to be of interest to your students. Learning about election can be a great comfort to them—it assures them that life has meaning and that we belong to God (John 10:27-29; Rom. 8:28-39).

PROCEDURE

Review Quiz

Answers to this week's fill-in-the blank quiz are as follows (allow for some variations):

1. there is one God in three distinct persons
2. the Great Commission (Matt. 28:19); the angel's announcement to Mary (Luke 1:35); Christ's baptism (Luke 3:21-22); Christ's announcement in the temple (Luke 4:18); the benediction (2 Corinthians 13:13).

3. God or truly and fully God or equally God

4.-5. incommunicable; communicable

6. the Bible

7-9. history; conscience; nature

10. breathed

Video Presentation

To the surprise of many teachers, election is a topic that teens often find interesting to discuss and explore. Pastor Lew's dramatic and clear presentation of this teaching (see, for example, his "Niagara Falls" example) should stimulate some good discussion. It will also probably give your teens a better handle on this topic than many adults have in the church today.

Ask your students to be alert to copy down the TULIP acronym near the end of the video.

OPTION

To help students focus on one question at a time, try stopping the video immediately after Pastor Lew's discussion of each of his six questions on election. This "stop and go" procedure will also help students more readily recall how Pastor Lew answered each question.

Video Discussion Guide

When you discuss today's questions, be especially sensitive to giving students opportunities to raise their own questions, objections, and other comments. Guidelines for today's discussion questions follow.

1. **What is God's election? Explain the doctrine of election from both the Calvinistic and the "free will" perspective. Which explanation gives humans more control? Which view do you personally think is right? Why?**

   Begin by recalling with the class the simple definition of election given on the video: God's choice to save some of the human race. Berkhof's definition is only slightly longer: "God's eternal purpose to save some of the human race in and by Jesus Christ" *(Manual of Christian Doctrine).*

   Take a moment to review the distinction between election and predestination, namely that predestination is the more inclusive of the two terms, covering all of God's decreeing and planning, whereas election applies more narrowly to God's decreeing salvation for some of the human race.

   Ask your students to explain the distinction between the Calvinistic and "free will" view of election. Emphasize that Calvinists believe that God chose us first, and because God chose us, he directs our lives in such a way that we believe in him. Those who believe in free will hold that God offers salvation to everyone; those who accept are the ones whom God chooses. The free will view gives humanity more control; the Calvinist explanation gives God more control.

   After you feel your group has an adequate grasp of what election is, ask them which view they personally think is right and why. Encourage them to be candid and open. Perhaps you can point out that the Calvinistic view is difficult for many people to accept because it seems to rob them of control.

OPTION

Read Article 16 of the Belgic Confession to help define election. Then ask the group to explain how election shows God's mercy and how it shows God's justice. You may want to refer to Pastor Lew's Niagara Falls illustration to help students understand this distinction.

TIP

Be aware that some of your students may come from a "free will" background. Others may personally prefer the "free will" view to the Calvinistic interpretation that their church teaches. When you make the case for election, be careful not to suggest that those who hold the free will view are somehow inferior Christians.

TIP

This is one of the best texts for defending the Calvinist interpretation of the doctrine of election. You may want to ask students to remember its location.

OPTION

You may want to talk about the texts cited by those who believe in free will. Here are a few: Joshua 24:25; John 3:16; John 7:27; Acts 16:31. The Calvinist, of course, would argue that those who chose to believe were able to do so only by God's previous choice to give them faith.

TIP

Your students may expect you to immediately say that of course election is fair. While you do want to affirm this, go out of your way to avoid prematurely closing off discussion in this way. Instead, invite candid responses, admit any doubts you may have, and listen carefully to what your students say.

2. **How do the following texts support the idea of election, of God's choosing some to be saved?**

   - **Ephesians 1:4-5:** These verses plainly say God "chose us in Christ before the foundation of the world. . . . He destined us for adoption as his children through Jesus Christ, according to the good pleasure of his will" (NRSV).
   - **Romans 8:28-30:** This passage restates the election theme so common in Paul's epistles.
   - **Matthew 24:22, 24, 31:** These verses, cited in the Perspective section of the session, indicate that Jesus used the term "the elect" to refer to God's people.
   - **John 15:16:** Jesus says to his disciples, "You did not choose me, but I chose you and appointed you to go and bear fruit. . . . "

3. **Do you think the teaching of election is fair? Why or why not?**

   Some in your group may say that they think it's cruel of God to save some but not others. Accept such comments, but gently point out that the human race really is bad enough to deserve universal condemnation (tragedies such as shootings in high schools are just one current example of this you may want to cite). Refer them once more to Pastor Lew's Niagara Falls illustration: we are all heading down the river, toward the falls, caught up in our own sin and evil. God, in his mercy, plucks some from the current and allows others to continue their headlong plunge into destruction. As Pastor Lew asks, "Can we accuse God of being unfair because he saves some and not all?"

   Dr. D. James Kennedy once said that there is one prayer you will never want to come from your lips: Lord, give me what I deserve! Only by grace does God choose to save any of us. God is God; we are humans.

   There is a great deal of wisdom in acknowledging that we are merely clay, and God is the potter (Rom. 9:20-21). In addition, much of who God is and what God does remains mysterious to us. Some things we simply cannot understand or explain.

4. **Does God choose to send some people to hell? And if so, isn't this cruel?**

   As the video points out, most Calvinists believe that God does not choose to send people to hell. People go to hell because they sin, not because God deliberately chooses to send them there. The only choosing that God does is to save some from their dreadful fate. Far from being cruel, God is full of love. His grace is amazing; his mercy boundless. Are firemen cruel for saving some—but not all—of the people in a burning building?

5. **How do you know if you're elect?**

   This question has plagued many people throughout the ages. The answer, says Pastor Lew, is profound yet simple. We believe that our hearts are totally dead toward God. The only way we will become even the least bit interested in him is if he begins to work in our hearts. And once he begins working in us, he never quits. So how can we be sure we're elect? Simply by asking ourselves if we believe in Jesus. If we do, we're elect. John 3:16 and countless other passages in Scripture clearly tell us so.

6. What does TULIP stand for?

The TULIP acronym is famous among Calvinists. While you won't have time to go into much detail, you can at least review what the letters stand for (use your board or newsprint so students can be sure they get it right).

T Total depravity. Every aspect of our being—our mind, body, will, and emotion—is tainted with sin. Note that this doctrine does not say that humans are as bad as they can be. We're not absolutely depraved. But we're unable to meet God's standards.

U Unconditional election. God's choosing who will be saved is not based on anything we do, but on his will.

L Limited atonement. Jesus died for those whom God has chosen.

I Irresistible grace. Once God has chosen us, we are unable to resist him; we can't turn him down.

P Perseverance of the saints. Once we believe, we cannot fall away from the faith; we're assured of salvation because God preserves us.

TIP

As adolescents seek to make their faith real and personal, they often need assurances that God loves and accepts them. In your discussion of election, take care to convey this to your class. Assure them that if they sense in their hearts a love for God or a desire for God, God wants them and is already at work in their hearts. And God never fails to save those whom he intends to save. Let your students know that even if they feel somewhat indifferent or hostile toward God right now, God may still have chosen them as his children and will begin to work to bring their faith alive.

Closing

Invite group members to reflect quietly for half a minute or so on how amazing it is that God chooses us to be his children! This awesome God—who made heaven and earth and all things—knows our names, loves us enough to send his Son to die for us, and chooses us to be his own forever. Let the group sense your own gratitude and awe. Then simply invite them to say a prayer of thanks to God for the gift of salvation in Christ. Invite those who feel indifferent or unsure to silently ask God to work in their hearts to give them his assurance of salvation.

OPTION

Being chosen by God means that we belong to our faithful Savior, Jesus Christ. Q&A 1 of the Heidelberg Catechism incomparably expresses what this means. Give students a copy of this much-loved question and answer, then read it together as part of your closing time.

If you sense that some students still have questions about election or are somehow bothered by today's session, give them a call sometime this week. Invite them out for a Coke and some talk. Who knows—God might use you and even a video lesson on election to touch someone's heart.

The Image of God

SCRIPTURE

Genesis 1:26-27, 31; Ephesians 4:20-24; Colossians 3:9-10

BELGIC CONFESSION

Article 14

PURPOSE

In today's video, the focus begins to change from God to humanity. Pastor Lew begins by talking about the various ways children often image or reflect their parents, then makes the transition to humanity imaging or reflecting God (Gen. 1:26; Belgic Confession, Article 14). Pastor Lew asks why non-Christians can often be very compassionate, loving, creative people. The answer is that they were made in the image of God and still reflect, in a broad sense, something of God's goodness, justice, morality, truth, beauty, and so on. They are somewhat like a perfect sheet of paper that has been crumpled up (but not destroyed). But only Christ-filled persons can image God in the narrow sense of the original perfection and beauty that God gave man and woman at creation. Christ works in our lives to restore the image of God in us to what it once was. In Christ, we are new creatures and can truly reflect something of God's knowledge, righteousness, and holiness.

After today's session, students should have a stronger sense of their own worth—and the worth of others—as imagebearers of God. They should be able to explain what it means for Christians and non-Christians to be images of God. They should be able to relate the image of God to themselves, to others, and to significant moral issues of our times.

PERSPECTIVE

A game we played as children was "Who Am I?" The leader had in mind a person we all knew. The others would ask questions to try to learn that person's identity. Only yes or no answers could be given.

Today, many people are still asking that question. Who or what am I? A child of nature, a chance product of the environment, here today and gone tomorrow? Does anyone out there care that I exist?

A tragedy of our time is that many young people answer that question negatively. No one cares; life holds no lasting meaning. Little wonder that some seek momentary satisfaction in sex, possessions, alcohol, or other drugs. When these fail, as they do, "calling it quits" looks appealing and the suicide rate soars.

There is an alternative to pessimism: the good news that we are made in God's image and that God knows and cares about each one of us. Though disturbed by sin, the image of God in us has not been obliterated; "small traces" can be discerned even in unbelievers, as the Belgic Confession says (Article 14). Those traces are a reminder of a better past—before the fall—and make us hope for a better future.

All the optimistic philosophies of human nature build on that remnant of the image of God that is still in us. From the Renaissance through the Enlightenment of the eighteenth century to the human-potential movement of the 1970s, those who preferred a positive view of mankind to the older emphasis on sin built on that hope. For centuries people emphasized that the human creature is an animal who *thinks.* That emphasis was to change—the counter-culture of the 1960s, Vietnam, totalitarianism, the atom bomb, world turmoil, terrorism, AIDS, and corruption at home made realists of millions of former optimists. Novelists, existentialist philosophers, and neo-orthodox theologians became convinced that in reality the human creature is an animal who *stinks.*

Because pessimism and cynicism are hard to live with, a search for alternatives goes on among the thoughtful, including the young and thoughtful. Many have turned to New Age ideas, postmodernist thinking, and even witchcraft. Others have become Christians. Earnest, and having wearied themselves with the placebos of our modern youth culture, they have found satisfaction in the gospel, and they want to pass it on.

Christianity offers a realistic appraisal of human nature. Calvinists especially should not be shaken at revelations of the foibles and moral lapses of celebrities or common folk. In this session we're reminded that humanity is not only "guilty and subject to physical and spiritual death" but also "wicked, perverse, and corrupt" (Belgic Confession, Article 14).

Pastor Lew discusses the theological problem of the nice people we all know who are not Christians; he relates this to what remains in us of God's image. God has not forsaken humanity; in his "common grace" he still blesses it. He loves his fallen creatures, restrains sin, and enables all people to do works of "civil righteousness." This is why "worldly" people can carry on so admirably by canons of common sense and decency and may even appear to be superior to many Christians. This is why science, government, and culture may flourish, and why there is an appreciation for the good, the true, and the beautiful outside the church.

Like Article 14 in the Belgic Confession, the Heidelberg Catechism teaches that we are "totally unable to do any good" unless we are born again (Q&A 8), and it limits doing "good" to Christians (Q&A 91). In his commentary, however, Ursinus, the author, says that he has in mind "saving" good, not works of civil righteousness. He thus qualifies his apparently harsh teaching of "total depravity" and takes the same position as De Brès in the Belgic Confession.

The church's teaching, as harsh as it may sound, offers an adequate explanation for the condition of humanity in our time. Your students are faced daily with the evidence of humanity's fallen nature. That the image of God exists in us, even in our imperfect state, points them to God's grace. The church's teaching about the image of God in us enables your students to answer positively the age-old question "Who am I?" The discussion guide summarizes the answer well: We are cherished children of the one we resemble.

PROCEDURE

Review Quiz

1. b
2. b
3. b
4. c
5. a
6. c
7. d
8. b
9. c
10. a

Video Presentation

Ask your students to listen for the phrase "image of God" and its two meanings (broad sense and narrow sense). Then play the video all the way through.

OPTION

Stop the video just after the paper-burning demonstration, when Pastor Lew asks if human beings are more like the burned paper or the crumpled paper. "What is the answer?" is the phrase to listen for. Invite students to state their choices and the reasons behind them. Then continue on with the video.

Video Discussion Guide

1. **Think of someone you know who probably isn't a Christian. Describe some of that person's positive qualities and gifts. According to Pastor Lew, what enables people like this to do good and to be loving, productive human beings?**

   Do students sense the dilemma that the video raises: How can those who don't know the Lord, whose hearts are darkened by sin, be such fine people? The answer Pastor Lew suggests is that, though damaged by sin, they are simply reflecting their Creator. They have not completely lost God's image or likeness.

TIP

Break the ice by describing a nonbeliever you know who has many gifts and fine qualities. Then ask for examples from the group.

2. **What do we mean when we say that we—and all people—are "images of God"?**

   To be an "image" of God is to be a likeness of God, to resemble God in somewhat the same way that children resemble their father and mother.

3. **Read Genesis 1:26-27, 31. How did humans resemble God at creation?**

   In the beginning humans resembled God in all his goodness (v. 31). Adam and Eve had the ability to obey God perfectly, to know God, and to reflect God's righteousness and holiness. As reflections of the divine King and Ruler, humankind was given dominion over all of God's creation. The resemblance between Father and children was unmistakable.

OPTION

Article 14, from which the video quotes one line, further elaborates on how humans initially resembled God ("good, just, holy, able by his own will to conform in all things to the will of God . . . in honor . . . excellence"). Take a couple of minutes to distribute copies of Article 14 and read the first four sections together.

In addition to the verses from Genesis, have students read Psalm 8, especially verses 5-8, which describe humanity's rule over all of creation.

OPTION

Invite the group to suggest other illustrations that show the "damaged but not destroyed" idea of the image of God in people. For instance, a car that's been in an accident and is dented and damaged but is still drivable, or a window that is dirty and cracked but not smashed.

4. **When sin entered the world, did people lose the image of God? How does the crumpled paper analogy help explain what happened?**

   Sin damaged and distorted the image of God in us but did not destroy it, as the crumpled paper analogy suggests. Just as the crumpled paper is still paper and able to be used as such, however imperfectly, so we are still images of God, though damaged by sin.

5. **Should Christians reflect God differently than non-Christians? Why or why not? See Ephesians 4:20-24 and Colossians 3:9-10.**

   Christians should reflect the true knowledge, righteousness, and holiness of God (the narrow sense of the image of God, as described in the passages listed). Why? Because Christians are constantly being regenerated and renewed by the Holy Spirit; they have put off the old self and have put on the new. They have a true knowledge of who God is. They are truly righteous through Jesus Christ. They are truly holy and are no longer controlled by sin and Satan. Because of their special relationship to God through Christ, they begin to reflect and image God as he originally intended.

6. **What impact can the "image of God" have on the way you see yourself and others? On your attitudes and behavior? Please complete the following statements:**

   - **Because all people are made in the image of God, I should . . .**
   - **Because I am made in the image of God and am becoming a new person in Christ, I should . . .**

   After providing a couple of minutes for writing, invite students to share their statements with the rest of the group. A couple of sample statements follow:

   - Because all people are made in the image of God, I should treat them with love and care and respect. I should try to avoid hurting others with my words or attitudes or actions. I should look for opportunities to praise and help people.
   - Because I am made in the image of God and am becoming a new person in Christ, I should see myself as a cherished child of the One I resemble. I should feel loved and valued and secure. I should not regard myself as worthless but as having great value in God's sight. I should want to be treated with respect and dignity.

TIP

Share your own candid statements with the group to promote their participation in this activity.

7. **Believing in the biblical teaching that people are imagebearers of God has some wide-reaching implications, especially for the ethical or social issues our society faces. For example, how might this belief affect your view of capital punishment? What other issues might be affected by believing that all people are made in the image of God?**

If we regard all people as imagebearers of God, then we will, generally speaking, want to preserve life rather than take it. In the case of capital punishment, we would need to carefully weigh whether taking the life of a murderer is required for taking the life of another imagebearer and for protecting society at large. We would need to seriously consider whether a life sentence with no possibility of parole would accomplish the same objectives.

Other issues involving imagebearing include abortion, euthanasia, war, gun control, violence, racism, poverty, genetic manipulation, and so on. In all these issues and more, Christians need to be concerned about protecting and enhancing the lives of others.

OPTION

Decide to spend time together on an issue that obviously concerns your group. Discuss possibilities as a group: inviting a guest speaker; writing letters to the editor of your local newspaper; taking some kind of direct action related to the issue.

Closing

At one point in today's video, Pastor Lew wonders whether others can see Jesus when they look at him. Invite your students to ask themselves this question for a moment. Can others see Jesus in their words, attitudes, and actions? After a moment of silence, invite students to pray silently, asking Jesus to shine through the details of their daily lives so that others may look at them and see the God they resemble. End the prayer yourself by thanking God for all the ways your students reflect their Lord and Savior.

OPTION

If your students know each other well, try this activity. Distribute notecards to your group. Each card should have one student's name written on the top. Students should write one way in which they see Jesus in the person whose name is at the top of the card. Pass the cards along until each student has a comment from each class member. Give each student her or his card to take home and read.

As part of your closing activity, divide into two groups and read Psalm 8 responsively.

Sin

SCRIPTURE

Psalm 51:1-12; Matthew 5:27-29; Romans 3:23; 5:12-19; 1 John 1:9

BELGIC CONFESSION

Articles 14 and 15

PURPOSE

Pastor Lew begins by raising four questions about sin. While it is possible for people to reduce the amount of actual sins or transgressions in their lives, he says, it is impossible for them to improve their sinful human nature, the "original sin" they inherited from Adam and Eve.

Pastor Lew then raises the question of exactly when a particular sequence of thoughts or actions becomes sin. He uses six chairs to represent various stages of sin. The first stage is knowing about a certain evil. The second stage is being curious about that evil. The third stage is desiring to do that evil. The fourth stage is lusting or strongly desiring to do the evil thing. The fifth stage is deciding to do the evil. The sixth stage is actually committing the sin. Pastor Lew says sin occurs during the last three stages. He concludes by again emphasizing that actual sins flow out of our fallen human nature, producing guilt and pollution in our lives.

After today's session, your students should be more aware of the process of sin in the ordinary events of their lives. They should be able to describe the six stages of sin and evaluate where sin occurs in their own actions. They should be able to define the terms listed above.

PERSPECTIVE

Any treatment of the doctrine of sin should pay its respects to Augustine (A.D. 354-430), who developed it for the church. The impetus for Augustine's extensive writings on sin and grace was the teaching of Pelagius, a sincere, mistaken monk mentioned in the Belgic Confession, and two of his friends. Believing that a just, good God would not make impossible demands of his creatures, these men held that if God said that we should live free from sin, we must have the ability to do it. Human nature is uncorrupted; its basic components, including the will, cannot be changed. The effect of the fall on mankind was only superficial—it set a bad example. We can will either good or evil; therefore, if we ought to be good, we can be.

The Pelagians meant well; they wanted people to live responsibly, to make good choices, and to honor God. But their insistence that freedom from sin in this life is a possibility led to a denial of the need for the grace of the Holy Spirit.

All this was sufficient to shake Augustine, but when the pope and a church council favored the Pelagian heresy, he doubled his efforts and turned out some of the finest work in the history of the church. He died while writing against his opponent Julian, a deposed bishop who had written that "by free will man is set free from God." Augustine held that even without sin we would be dependent on the Almighty; we are much more so in our present predicament. Julian believed that the will has full ability to decide as it pleases and carries the rest of human nature with it. This same view was to reappear in Erasmus's writing against Luther and in the Arminians at Dort, and it is widely held today.

In their discussion about sin your students will also be indirectly dealing with the question of free will. What is the will? Is it free? If so, in what sense? What is the relation of the will to the rest of human nature? These questions lie at the heart of our session.

The issue is whether humanity is presently in a normal or abnormal state. Like it or not, the Bible teaches that our condition is abnormal. As a human race, we are not what we once were or ought to be. We are sinners in need of grace. This is the great offense of the "natural human." The doctrine of sin is difficult to accept, for it levels our pride, but it is fundamental; the whole Bible presupposes it. That is why the Bible is a history of salvation. Weaken the doctrine of sin and you weaken the doctrine of salvation also. Jesus came to seek and to save those who are lost.

The reason that we are all involved in sin is that we are one family. "Sin entered the world through one man . . . and in this way death came to all . . . because all sinned" (Rom. 5:12). There was a time when our first parents and the human race were one. They fell and we fell with them. That is the simple, weighty biblical teaching, and it squares with what we see in life. Humanity is falling all the time: we don't need to look far to find the sins of hatred, deceit, stealing, or self-interest. If we think that we are free of these, what about our "secret" sins: lack of love, indifference, pride, ingratitude? Although no one denies the mess the world is in, not all see it as sin against God. But that is exactly what makes sin sin.

The Belgic Confession says that sin "is a corruption of all nature—an inherited depravity which even infects small infants in their mother's womb. . . . Sin constantly boils forth as though from a contaminated spring" (Article 15). This is not a pretty teaching, and some reject it for that reason. Our concern is whether or not it is true. Why is it necessary for us to be born again if we are to see the kingdom of God, as Jesus said (John 3:3)? Are we Pelagian at heart until we are transformed by the Spirit of God?

Our solidarity in sin is so real and all-embracing that we lack solidarity in anything else. Look at our world. Human beings are pitted against each other more terribly than anything possible in the lower creations. Made like God but alienated from him, humans are also alienated from themselves, and no human panacea improves their condition. Those who wince at this teaching should study Romans 1:18-20 and then take a long look at the world.

Interestingly, and as though to sustain us after pondering sin, the Belgic Confession sets the covenant of grace alongside inherited sin. The reason that baptism is interjected is the Roman Catholic teaching that baptism cleanses from all sin. In 1546 the Council of Trent stated, against the Reformers' teaching, that while Christ removes the guilt of sin, sin's corrupting influence remains. Two years after the Belgic Confession was written the Council of Trent closed with further blasts at the Reformation; its catechism condemned the notion that after baptism the root of sin is still left in the soul (QXLI).

Most Reformed theologians would agree with Pastor Lew's teaching about sin, and certainly about its importance. But some might disagree with his opinion that the third chair is not included in the act of sin. In the video discussion guide, students are asked what they think—they'll certainly be interested in your opinion too.

PROCEDURE

Review Quiz

Here are the answers to today's true/false quiz. Be sure to have students correct all false answers when going over the quiz.

1. true
2. false (God created Adam and Eve in his image as good, holy creatures)
3. false (unbelievers retain something of the image of God in its broad aspects)
4. true
5. true
6. true
7. true
8. false (total depravity)
9. false (this is the "free will" position)
10. false (people know they're elect because they believe in Jesus)

Video Presentation

As they watch today's video, have students jot down definitions of the words listed in their session guides (Video Discussion Guide, #1). Ask them to also jot down the names of the six stages of sin (#2) as Pastor Lew presents them on the video.

TIP

How are students doing with the quiz section of the session? For variation, you might ask students to take turns giving the questions and answers to the class. Every now and then throw in some of your own fun questions. If some students are consistently having trouble with the quizzes, consider doing them in small groups of two or three students each, then reviewing answers with the entire group.

TIP

Before showing today's video, stimulate some interest among your students by asking when something becomes a sin. For example, if we only think about cheating on a test, are we sinning? If we really *want* to cheat on a test, is that sin? If we decide to cheat on tomorrow's test, is that sin? Or must we actually cheat on the test before it becomes sin? Solicit student opinions and explain that the video will help answer these questions.

OPTION

Stop the video after Pastor Lew lists the four questions about sin (near the beginning). He says that all questions can be answered with both a yes and a no. Talk with your students about how this can be. Do they have any explanations of how, on the one hand, we can apparently reduce the amount of sin in our lives, but on the other hand, doing so is totally impossible? Some may be able to guess the distinction between actual sins and original sin that Pastor Lew explains later in the video. Listen to your students' explanations, if any, and continue with the video.

TIP

The video doesn't provide a separate caption to define "original sin," as it does with the other terms in this lesson; rather, it shows the term as it is used in Article 14 of the Belgic Confession. You may want to distribute and read Article 14 when talking about original sin.

TIP

Pastor Lew briefly mentions another term in today's video: *total depravity.* You may want to review its definition with your group. It refers to our inability to please God on our own with our sinful human nature. It also refers to the way sin has tainted every aspect of our nature (see comments on original sin).

OPTION

Divide students into small groups of two or three. Ask each group to dramatize the six stages of sin. They should choose a situation in which someone is tempted (the video mentions a couple—ask the groups to take fresh examples), then act it out, showing how the person who is tempted moves from knowledge to action.

Video Discussion Guide

1. Definitions:

Although most of the definitions are flashed on the screen, your students may not have adequate time to write them all down accurately. Review and amplify the eight definitions as you think necessary.

a. **original sin:** the sin of Adam and Eve passed on to you and to me. (You may want to have the class read Romans 5:12-19, which clearly describes original sin.) The doctrine of original sin shows us that sin is universal—no one escapes it—and that it keeps on reproducing from generation to generation.

b. **actual sins:** the wrong things (transgressions) we do every day. This is the sin referred to in Romans 3:23, which you may want the class to look up.

c. **sins of omission:** things we should do but don't. These are sins of neglect, of failing to do something we should have done. They are a form of transgression or actual sins.

d. **sins of commission:** wrong things we do. Again, this is a form of transgression or actual sins.

e. **guilt:** our legal standing before God. We have violated God's law, stand guilty before him, and deserve punishment. Because of our sin against God and our legal standing of being guilty, we usually also *feel* guilty.

f. **pollution:** our dirty condition because of our sin. Like an open sewer, sin has "seeped into every part of our lives, staining and spoiling thoughts, words, deeds, feelings, and inclinations" (Cornelius Plantinga, *A Sure Thing*).

2. Name the six stages in the "process of sin."

The six stages of sin could be described in one word each, as follows:

- Stage 1: knowledge
- Stage 2: curiosity
- Stage 3: desire
- Stage 4: lust (strong desire)
- Stage 5: decision or choice
- Stage 6: action

3. At which of the six stages do you think sin occurs?

Pastor Lew says sin usually occurs in the last three stages, beginning with strong desire, proceeding to choosing to do the sin, and culminating in actually doing it.

See if your students agree with this. They'll probably want to know your opinion too. For scriptural support of the idea that sin begins with the "lust" stage, see

Matthew 5:27-29: "Anyone who looks at a woman lustfully has already committed adultery with her in his heart."

4. **Think of some recent sin in your life. Did it follow these six stages?**

   With this question, the issue of sin becomes very personal. Let your students know that they need not share their answers with the group.

   You may want to point out the six stages of one of your own past sins. Then invite students to give examples if they wish or raise any related questions they have.

5. **On a scale of one to ten, with ten being very seriously and one not at all, how seriously does our society in general regard sin?**

   Let the kids jot down a number on their session guide, then quickly go around and share what they wrote. Talk with the group about the view of sin kids get from the movies and TV programs they watch, from the music they listen to, from sports and entertainment leaders, and from politicians. Do they agree that sin is tolerated, pooh-poohed, or even glamorized? Or do they see our society taking it more seriously? If the former, what do they think causes us to take a "lite" view of sin?

6. **Why not simply avoid the topic of sin? Why study something so negative and depressing?**

   Ask group members to offer their own reasons for studying sin. A knowledge of sin and how it works is important for Christians. The more we understand sin, the quicker we can spot it in our own lives and fight against it. And when we're aware of our sin, we can confess it to God and be forgiven for it.

Closing

The session should be ended on a positive note of forgiveness of sins in Christ.

Here are some suggestions:

- Call on several students to read Romans 5:12-19, which contrasts death through Adam with life through Christ.
- Read Psalm 51:1-12 responsively as a prayer.
- Read the promise of forgiveness in 1 John 1:9.
- Bow in silent prayer, asking God for forgiveness of personal sins. Finish the silent prayer time yourself by thanking God for his forgiveness through Jesus Christ.

Salvation

SCRIPTURE

Psalm 38; Acts 3:19; 16:13-15; Romans 5:1-2, 9; 1 Thessalonians 2:12; 2 Timothy 3:15; 1 Peter 5:10

BELGIC CONFESSION

Articles 17 and 23

PURPOSE

Today's video explains the first four "steps" in the process of salvation (calling, regeneration, conversion, justification). Pastor Lew begins with a review of guilt and pollution, noting that these result in alienation—a chasm between God and us. Pastor Lew then returns to the four questions he raised last time and gives a simple illustration of how we are "dirty on the inside" and unable to remove our sinful human nature, no matter how hard we try.

Salvation is a way out of the alienation produced by sin. First God *calls* us—he puts an "internal ear" in our hearts so we can hear his external call through the words of other Christians, through instruction, and so on. Second God makes our dead hearts come alive again in the process known as *regeneration.* Third, with God's help, we respond in faith and repentance, and begin to turn our lives around *(conversion).* We respond to God in faith and repentance. Fourth, God *justifies* us, declaring us not guilty and making us right with him. (Next week we'll look at the final step in the process—sanctification.)

After today's session, your students should be more aware of and appreciative of how God is working in their own lives for their salvation. They should be able to describe the first four steps in the process of salvation and to reflect on the nature of these steps in their own lives.

PERSPECTIVE

Sessions 10 and 11 cover steps in the "order of salvation," as Reformed theology calls it. The arrangement of steps in that "order" may vary. Some writers prefer a logical order; others, one that is chronological. Still others hesitate to make any listings of steps and think in terms of a many-sided figure, each side representing some aspect of the work of the Holy Spirit in us. In the center of the figure is union with Christ, which gives meaning to it all. In this series the steps are discussed in two sessions, four steps in this one and one in the next. Election, also "in Christ" (Eph. 1:4), has already been discussed; now we turn our attention to calling, regeneration, conversion, and justification.

Calling, as Pastor Lew says, is twofold: sometimes it is set forth as the proclamation of the gospel, the call to repent and believe; elsewhere calling is "internal," or "effectual." Thus, not only are many "invited" (Matt. 22:14) but some who receive that outward call are effectually called as well (2 Tim. 1:9; 1 Cor. 1:26; Heb. 31; 1 Pet. 2:9). In these latter instances calling is not only an invitation but the mysterious opening of the heart by God so that it is ready to hear him. Before, the heart was rebellious, going its own way; after God's internal call, it willingly obeys him. Some other passages that deal with "calling" are Rom. 8:28-30; 9:12, 24; 1 Tim. 6:12; Phil. 3:14.

Another stage in salvation is regeneration. Jesus repeatedly stated that rebirth is necessary for entrance into the kingdom of God (John 3:3, 5-8). Because of the nature and effects of sin, a complete change is necessary if we are to become children of God; "flesh gives birth to flesh, but the Spirit gives birth to spirit" (see John 1:13; Eph. 2:1-5; 4:22-24; Rom. 6:13; 1 Pet. 1:23; 2:9; Tit. 3:5; 2 Cor. 5:17; Gal. 6:15; James 1:18). Although regeneration is suggested in the Old Testament (Deut. 30:6; Jer. 13:23; Ezek. 11:19; 36:26; 37:14), it was not elaborated until the accomplishment of redemption in Christ and at Pentecost.

Regeneration is beyond human understanding. It is the gift of a new life in which the controlling principle is holiness. Those who deny God's sole agency, claiming that the human will cooperates and that regeneration and conversion are synonymous, deny the radical nature of sin and the sovereignty of grace. The fact is, only God's Spirit can give new life to those dead in sin. Believing that, we place our confidence in him.

Although Reformed theology teaches that we are passive in regeneration, it does not make the same claim about conversion. Abraham Kuyper pointed out that the Bible refers to conversion as an act of the Holy Spirit only six times; a hundred and forty-four times as our own. We have an active role in conversion: it is our responsibility, according to Scripture, to turn to the Lord. Of course, we can only do so because God has regenerated us, has given us the Spirit, and has given us faith.

So conversion consists of both repentance and faith; it is a conscious forsaking of the old life of sin and the beginning of a new way of life in Christ. The "old has [indeed] gone, the new has come" (2 Cor. 5:17). That change must occur, sooner or later, in every child of God. In this session, your class will have the opportunity to discuss their own spiritual journeys. As the video discussion guide points out, conversion can be dramatic or gradual. Your students can be assured that the Holy Spirit continues to work in each of their hearts.

By faith we are justified; justification means being accepted, having proper standing with God. "When the kindness and love of God our Savior appeared, he saved us, not because of righteous things we had done, but because of his mercy . . . so that, having been justified by his grace, we might become heirs" (Tit. 3:4-7). The "good news" of the Bible is that salvation is free. We "are justified freely by [God's] grace through the redemption that came by Christ Jesus" (Rom. 3:24). Justification does not mean that God observes how well we have done and then declares us to be fit citizens of his kingdom. Rather, he justifies sinners (Rom. 5:6, 9-11, 16-21).

The foundation of justification is atonement. Jesus offered the only possible and acceptable sacrifice for sin, and it is his righteousness that is credited to believers (Rom. 3:21ff.; Phil. 3:9). Justification, then, is a judicial act of God by which sinners are accounted righteous before God's law on the basis of the merits of Christ. Our "hope is built on nothing less than Jesus' blood and righteousness."

PROCEDURE

Review Quiz

1. false (This early stage is generally not considered sinful. This would be a good time to review all six stages of sin described in the last session: knowledge, curiosity, desire, lust, decision, action.)
2. true
3. true
4. false (original sin is the sin of Adam and Eve passed on to you and me)
5. false (sins of omission describe things we should have done but failed to do)
6. true
7. true
8. true
9. true
10. false (Christians are in the process of reflecting God's image more completely but they haven't yet arrived at perfection)

Video Presentation

Explain that the next two sessions will focus on how we become Christians. Then distribute notecards and invite students to jot down any questions they might have about how we come to Jesus. These needn't be only "process" questions about what happens first or what God does and what we do; questions about our own experiences, our own spiritual journeys are also welcome; for instance, How do I know if I'm saved? Is it OK to have doubts? What if I don't spend much time praying or reading the Bible? Why is it hard for me to trust God when things aren't going right? Collect the unsigned cards, read the questions aloud, and then make every attempt to deal with the questions in this session or in a future session. In fact, you may want to forego using today's session guide. Instead, simply show the video then deal with the students' questions.

Proceed to play the video through without stopping.

TIP

Today's session covers a lot of theological territory: alienation, God's call, regeneration, conversion, and justification. You'll want to keep an eye on the clock and cut back on some questions, if need be (consider, for example, skipping the usual review quiz). Also, do your best to apply those theological concepts to the feelings and experiences of your students. We've given you some suggestions about how to do that throughout the session.

Video Discussion Guide

1. **What is it like to feel alienated from God because of your sin? Why is it so important to our salvation to experience the alienation that sin causes?**

   To feel alienated from God is to feel that God is distant, that there is an uneasy silence between us and God, and that we are struggling alone with a great burden of guilt. Experiencing this alienation is crucial to our salvation. If we don't

OPTION

Read Psalm 38 for a telling description of David's struggle with guilt and alienation.

TIP

You can make this question more concrete by telling your group about your feelings when you were unable to pray or felt distant from God because you were struggling with the guilt of unconfessed sin. You needn't go into details, but if you can speak authentically about your feelings of alienation from God, you'll help your students come to terms with similar feelings. They'll see you as someone who, like them, is still on a spiritual journey, with all of its ups and downs.

OPTION

Read through Belgic Confession Article 17 with your class, noting how God sets out to find and to save fallen humanity, beginning with Adam and Eve and continuing until Christ returns. God is on our trail and will not stop until he catches us!

sense any separation from God because of our sins, we won't feel any need for salvation. This doesn't mean, of course, that we must go around in a constant depression because of our sin, or that we must feel separated from God a great deal of the time. Remind the class that Christ bridged the gap and brought God and us together again. But we do need to sense the damage that sin does to our relationship with God and others and to ourselves.

2. God's calling us is the first step in the process of salvation (see 1 Peter 5:10 and 1 Thessalonians 2:12). As you think about your own spiritual journey, what are some of the ways God has called or is calling you?

You may want to read the two passages mentioned above. Be sure to stress that God makes the first move (as we learned in the "election" session a few weeks ago). This is in contrast to the Arminian view held by many churches that we take the first step by accepting or rejecting God's offer of salvation.

Invite students to give examples of how God calls us externally (by the teaching and example of parents, friends, and other Christians; by what we learn at church or youth group; by life circumstances that drive us to ask for God's help; by the insight and understanding we gain as we read the Bible or listen to a sermon; and so on). When we truly "hear" these calls from God, it is because God has also called us internally, making us *want* to listen to the external means he is using.

3. What is the second step of salvation, and what does it mean (see Acts 16:13-15)?

The second step of salvation is regeneration. To regenerate means to make alive again. This happens when the Holy Spirit enters the dead heart of a sinner and begins to give it new life. Louis Berkhof defines regeneration as "that act of God by which the principle of the new life is implanted in man, and the governing disposition of the soul is made holy" (*A Manual of Christian Doctrine*). Berkhof distinguishes between internal calling and regeneration by calling the former a kind of "restricted" regeneration that "enables man to hear the call of God to the salvation of the soul." Regeneration in the broader sense occurs when "God's call is brought home effectively to the heart, so that man hears and obeys."

You may want to read Acts 16:13-15 as an example of regeneration. The passage tells of the conversion of Lydia and includes this evidence of her regeneration: "The Lord opened her heart to respond to Paul's message."

4. What is the third step of salvation, who performs it, and what are its two parts (see Acts 3:19)?

The third step of salvation is conversion. Conversion means to turn around. According to Berkhof, conversion is "the resulting conscious act of the regenerated sinner, whereby he, through the grace of God, turns to God in repentance and faith" (*Systematic Theology*). Whereas the first two steps are performed solely by God, this step centers on our response to God. With God's help, we take the difficult step of turning our lives around.

Talk with your group about what it means to have faith (note the three parts mentioned on the video: knowing what we believe, agreeing or believing that these things are true, and trusting in Jesus for our salvation. Repentance means being truly sorry for our sins, turning away from them, and turning to God. It is sometimes used to mean "conversion," as in Q&A 88 of the Heidelberg Catechism.

Acts 3:19 nicely sums up the conversion process. Be sure to read it with the group.

OPTION

Help students understand just how difficult conversion can be by sharing Cornelius Plantinga's description: "We are like a small outboard fishing boat headed downstream toward a ruinous waterfall. Our tendency is to let the stream carry us. That's easiest, especially if we don't know or care about the danger. We tend to go with the flow. Repentance [conversion] in such a process is a hard and delicate move. We have to see our danger, shift into reverse, plow stern-first backwards till we get upstream to quieter water. Then we have to turn carefully around and head against the current" (*A Sure Thing*).

5. **Must we all "be converted" to be saved? If conversion is a turn-around in our lives, must we be able to point to a specific time when we were converted? Explain.**

   Yes, we must all turn from sin and turn to God (be converted) to be saved. But the "turn-around" in Christian conversion can be dramatic or gradual. It is not necessary to be able to point to the specific day and hour.

   If students are familiar with the Bible, have them give some biblical examples of the sudden, dramatic variety of conversion (Paul, Lydia, Philippian jailer). Ask them for some contemporary examples too, and note that God sometimes uses crises in our lives to turn us noticeably toward him and away from sin. The main biblical example of a gradual conversion is that of Timothy (2 Tim. 3:15), who apparently was a Christian from childhood.

6. **You are at a Christian youth convention with other teens from your church and hundreds of other kids from all around the country. At the last big meeting of the conference, a guest speaker delivers a powerful appeal for people to come to the front and give their lives to Jesus Christ. You find yourself strangely moved. Something inside is tugging at you, urging you to join the others who are coming forward. At the same time you feel reluctant because you know you already are a Christian and have already given your life to Christ.**

   In this situation, what would you probably do? Why?

   As you listen to student responses, be sure to mention the legitimacy of recommitting one's life to Christ and of experiencing many "mini-conversions" throughout life. Answering an altar call could be a faith-building experience for some people.

   Also talk about the intense emotional element in many altar calls. Christians should avoid seeking out "spiritual highs" simply to put some excitement into an otherwise drab faith life.

7. Describe the fourth step along the way of salvation (see Romans 5:1-2, 9).

The fourth step is justification. Read the verses from Romans 5 and together review the definition of justification. It is a legal term, an act of God whereby he declares us not guilty (just as if we'd never sinned) on the basis of Christ's righteousness. It takes away our sins and gives us Christ's righteousness instead. It has the wonderful effect of making us God's sons and daughters.

Justification follows necessarily from God's call. When God calls us to be his own, he must provide a way for us to be declared righteous before him. Although we are spiritually bankrupt, God graciously credits the righteousness of Christ to our account.

TIP

Be careful when talking about justification not to make God the Father into a stern judge who is eager to give us the eternal punishment we so richly deserve, only to be kept from doing so by a loving Jesus. Remind the group that God himself sent Jesus to be our substitute. So in justification, we see not only the Father's justice satisfied but also his love expressed.

OPTION

Justification is the focus of Article 23 of the Belgic Confession. If you wish, have students take turns reading it.

Closing

If your group has grown fairly close over the first few weeks of this course, consider asking if anyone would be willing to say a few words about his or her conversion, be it gradual or more dramatic. Begin by saying a few things about your own spiritual pilgrimage; then warmly invite others to participate.

Close with a round of voluntary sentence prayers, focusing on thanks for the specific ways God used to call us to him in faith and repentance (Christian home, church, teachers, friends, the Bible, and so on).

TIP

If students are reluctant to participate, simply invite them to take a moment of silence and reflect on how God called them (or is calling them today) and how they responded (or are responding today).

Sanctification

SCRIPTURE

1 Corinthians 6:10; 12:27-31; 2 Corinthians 5:17; Galatians 5:22-26; Ephesians 4:20-32; James 2:14-17

BELGIC CONFESSION

Article 24

PURPOSE

Today's video begins with a review of the four steps of salvation discussed in session 10. Pastor Lew then defines the fifth step, sanctification, as the Spirit working in us to clean up the pollution caused by sin and to help us live the new life. He cites several passages that urge believers to live a life worthy of their calling, a life marked by good works and the fruit of the Spirit. Two versions of a story illustrate the difference between doing good works because we have to and doing them because we want to out of gratitude for what Christ has done for us. After reading part of Article 24, which describes the process of sanctification and the place of good works, Pastor Lew tells another story illustrating the importance of commitment and integrity in our spiritual lives. He concludes by challenging us to live in a way that reflects our faith.

After this session, your students should be motivated to live the "new life" in Christ. They should be able to define sanctification, tell why we do good works, list all five steps of the salvation process, and choose one or more "good works" to do during the coming week.

PERSPECTIVE

Before the Reformation, faith was defined as knowledge with assent. The church's teaching also distinguished explicit from implicit faith. The latter was said to be "faith in truths not known" by ordinary believers but known by the "teaching church," that is, the clergy. Laypeople were told to believe whatever the church teaches. The Reformers attacked this instruction, claiming that faith includes trust as well as knowledge and assent. In addition, Calvin and many Reformed leaders included obedience. To them faith meant accepting Christ as Savior *and* Lord, and that meant trying to do his will. This understanding of faith accounts for the accent in Reformed theology on sanctification, good works, and the law of God (see Heidelberg Catechism, Q&A 64, 86, 114, 115; Belgic Confession, Article 24). As we shall see in this session, Reformed faith is not passive and quiescent, but rather restless, active, yearning to please God.

Justification is one side of the coin of our salvation; sanctification is the other. Sanctification is the work of the Holy Spirit by which we are freed from sin and God's image is restored in us. It is the continuous cooperation of the Holy Spirit and the regenerated person to bring new life to maturity and enable us to begin to do God's will. Whereas justification is objective, its counterpart, sanctification, is subjective, a work "within." Together they recognize that sin necessitates "the double cure," the cancellation of guilt and reinstatement into divine favor, and the subjective elimination of sin. Salvation is complete when we are pardoned and cleansed.

Achieving "entire sanctification" in this life is impossible. That teaching, promoted by some "holiness churches," is unbiblical and dangerous; it is based on a superficial understanding of the holiness of God and the exceeding sinfulness of humanity. Sanctification—the work of the Holy Spirit in the believer's heart—is a part of all true Christian experience. Paul wrote that "if anyone does not have the Spirit of Christ, he does not belong to Christ" (Rom. 8:9).

As "the author and perfecter of our faith" (Heb. 12:2), Christ keeps us in union with himself forever. We were predestined, called, and justified, the apostle Paul wrote; we are also being sanctified and preserved, and we will be glorified (Rom. 8:30).

The doctrine of sanctification raises the issue of the place of good works in the Christian life. Article 14 of the Belgic Confession expresses concern for the necessity of good works in those who have "new life" and explains the ground of good works (faith), their nature as the fruit of "faith working through love," their source (God himself), and their imperfect nature.

The Reformers placed great emphasis on living out the faith in daily life. Justification and sanctification, though distinguished, are not to be separated in theory or in practice. We are saved "by grace . . . through faith . . . [as] the gift of God—not by works, so that no one can boast. For we are God's workmanship, created in Christ Jesus to do good works, which God prepared in advance for us to do" (Eph. 2:8-10).

The Heidelberg Catechism states the need for good works in a memorable question and answer (86):

> **We have been delivered from our misery by God's grace alone through Christ and not because we have earned it: why then must we still do good?**
>
> To be sure, Christ has redeemed us by his blood.
> But we do good because
> Christ by his Spirit is also renewing us to be like himself,
> so that in all our living
> we may show that we are thankful to God for all he has done for us,
> and so that he may be praised through us.
> And we do good
> so that we may be assured of our faith by its fruits,
> and so that by our godly living
> our neighbors may be won over to Christ.

The words "we do good so that we may be assured of our faith by its fruits" led to much introspection in some Reformed circles and the idea that salvation rested on one's fruit or works rather than on Christ. However, the intention of the Bible and the Heidelberg Catechism, as well as the Belgic Confession, is not to have us look at our good deeds for assurance of salvation, but at Christ, in whom we find it. The deeds are confirming evidence that we belong to him.

Are works necessary for salvation? Indeed they are, as the fruit of faith. Works are not part of the ground of salvation, but its living proof. The parable of the sheep and the goats makes clear the importance of good works and the natural manner in which they are done (Matt. 25:31-46). Yet even the best of these works is imperfect. Relying on them, we would have no peace. Instructed by God, however, we look to Christ and joyfully work out our salvation.

PROCEDURE

Review Quiz

Answers to today's fill-in-the-blank quiz are as follows. Be sure to allow for variations on some answers.

1. God's call
2. external
3. Regeneration

4-5. Conversion; repentance

6-8. justification; not guilty or innocent; Christ's taking our place and dying for our sins

9. election
10. action

Video Presentation

As you show today's video, consider stopping it just after Pastor Lew tells the story of the boy who broke his neighbor's window (before the cut-away to responses from the two students in Pastor Lew's group). Invite your students to give their ideas of what the story (with its two endings) means for our spiritual lives (see question 2 below). Then play the video and listen to the explanations of the story from the teens in Pastor's Lew group.

Video Discussion Guide

1. **Describe the fifth step in the process of salvation (see 2 Corinthians 5:17). Who performs this step (see 1 Corinthians 6:10; Ephesians 4:22-24)?**

   The fifth step in the process of salvation is sanctification: growing into a new and beautiful child of God, getting rid of the pollution of sin in our lives, and living a new life. "Therefore, if anyone is in Christ, he is a new creation; the old has gone, the new has come!" (2 Cor. 5:17). It is, as the Heidelberg Catechism puts it, "Christ by his Spirit renewing us to be like himself, so that in all our living

OPTION

Have the class read the first six lines of Article 24—it's a great summary of the process of salvation. Ask your students to pick out phrases that describe God's calling, regeneration, conversion, and sanctification. Note that in the entire salvation process, the Holy Spirit is at work.

we may show that we are thankful to God for all that he has done for us" (Q&A 86).

Have your group look up 1 Corinthians 6:10 and Ephesians 4:22-24. The former clearly states that sanctification is the work of the Holy Spirit in our hearts; the latter tells us to "put off the old self and put on the new self." So here, and throughout Scripture, sanctification is a process made possible by the work of the Spirit in us; but it's also a process in which we are active participants.

Take a moment to ask about the differences between justification and sanctification. Note that justification is a one-time act of God; sanctification is a continuous process in which we—with the help of the Holy Spirit—become more Christ-like and holy.

Mention to your group that there's a final, sixth step in the process of salvation that we'll be talking about later in the course when we discuss the church and the end times. Let your group guess what this step is. It's the step of glorification—going to be with the Lord we serve (see Rom. 8:30).

2. Recall the story (with two different endings) Pastor Lew told about the boy who bounced his ball through the window of his neighbor's house. What does this story have to say about our reason for "doing good?"

If you've already covered this question by stopping the video (see comments under video presentation, above), move on to question 3. As Pastor Lew explains on the video, in the first story ending, the boy must work to pay off the debt he owes his neighbor. If he wants to enjoy the friendship of his neighbor, he must work in the garden to pay off the bill for fixing the window. He works because he has to. In spiritual terms, there's a kind of "works righteousness" going on here; implied is the idea that what we do somehow helps pay off the debt of our sins.

In the second ending of the story, the boy's debt has been completely paid by the neighbor's son. But the boy continues to work in the garden simply because he wants to. He's grateful for the grace that was shown to him and he wants to show his gratitude by working. In spiritual terms, this represents why we as forgiven sinners do good works. Not to earn our salvation, but to express our joy at being forgiven. Not because we have to but because we want to. In fact, we can't help but do good works (see next question).

TIP

Ouch! This passage pulls no punches. "No works, no faith," it plainly says. Your teens need to hear this message along with the rest of us. But if you're noticing a kind of pained silence in your room about now, please take a moment to acknowledge that all of us are in the *process* of being sanctified, of becoming more Christ-like. We still struggle. We still sin. We still often prefer to take the easy way out and avoid the work of "doing good." Include some personal comments here, if you wish, about your own struggle to do good. Let your students hear (again!) that God is a forgiving Father. Let them hear that we're not in this sanctification business by ourselves. God 's Spirit is working in our hearts to produce evidence of our faith, even now.

3. Can a person be a Christian without doing anything that could be called "good" in God's sight? Can we have faith but not have a Christian lifestyle that goes with it?

Listen to your students' responses, and then have everyone look up James 2:14-17. The passage couldn't say it any clearer: "Faith, by itself, if not accompanied by action, is dead."

Talk about how once the Holy Spirit enters our hearts, we will naturally want to do good. In fact, we will have no real choice. "So, then, it is impossible for this holy faith to be unfruitful in a human being," says Article 24.

Luther once said that humanity is justified (declared righteous) by faith alone, but not by a faith that is alone. Genuine faith will produce good works. Where there are no good works, there is likely no genuine faith.

OPTION

Article 24 of the Belgic Confession addresses the reason why we do good works. As a follow-up to question 3, have students take turns reading aloud from it. Note especially the lines that clearly say good works do not contribute to our salvation: "Yet they do not count toward our justification—for by faith in Christ we are justified. . . . So then, we do good works, but not for merit—for what would we merit?"

4. **In many places the Bible tells us that our new lives in Christ should "bear fruit" and give evidence in our daily lives of the faith we claim to have (see, for example, 1 Corinthians 12:27-31; James 2:14; Ephesians 4:20-32; Galatians 5:22-26). Using these passages and your own ideas, work with one or two others to create a profile of what we as new people in Christ should be like. Write your ideas on a large sheet of paper—add some creative touches to your poster too.**

   Give each small group a large sheet of paper (newsprint or poster paper) and markers. Encourage them to be creative and have fun as they sketch their profiles of what "Joe and Jane Christian" should look like if they are living the "new life in Christ."

   The passages should give them plenty of ideas. Galatians mentions five fruits of the Spirit, and Ephesians 4 (cited on the video) urges us to be truthful, to avoid anger, to work hard, to build each other up with our words, to be kind and forgiving. First Corinthians 12:27-31 urges us to use our gifts for the benefit of the whole body of believers. Encourage the groups to use their own ideas as well as those they find in the listed passages.

   After about ten minutes, have the groups display and present their posters to the rest of the class.

TIP

Alert the groups when half of the allotted time is up, then again when they have a minute or two to go. Encourage groups to add a caption to their posters.

5. **What's the point of Pastor Lew's story about the soldier and the meeting in the train station?**

   Like the soldier, we need to be followers of Jesus who are committed to him and who act with integrity, even if it goes against our wishes. Did your students like the story? Is it a good reminder for us?

6. **OK, so you've heard about the need to be like Jesus and to show that we love him by doing good to others. If you're willing, list two or three "good works" that you could realistically do in the next week or so out of gratitude for what God has done for you. Be as specific as possible.**

   Before students who wish to do so make their lists, comment that often our best acts are done spontaneously as the need arises. But sometimes we need the discipline of planning to do specific acts of good. Give students a couple of minutes to make their lists, encouraging them to be realistic (listing things we have no intention of doing is a waste of time).

OPTION

Invite students to tell one other student about their commitment and to ask that student to remind them of the commitment at the next meeting. This will add a measure of accountability to what otherwise might well be forgotten or neglected.

OPTION

As a substitute closing, quickly review the five steps of the salvation process and ask your students to reflect for a moment on where they are in this process. Are they being called by God? If so, have they been given new life by the Spirit, and are they now "right with God? Are they working with the Holy Spirit to become more Christlike?

After a moment or two, invite students to share their responses with the group if they wish. Close by thanking God for reaching out to us, for walking with us on our spiritual journey, and for God's promise never to leave us.

Closing

Invite group members to look at their lists, then choose one item and make a commitment to actually doing that before class next week as a way of expressing gratitude to God. For your closing prayer, invite each person to silently ask God's help in fulfilling his or her commitment to action. Conclude the prayer yourself, thanking God for the great gift of salvation, and asking God to give you and your students a grateful faith that will naturally produce good works.

Perseverance of the Saints

SCRIPTURE

John 6:37-40; Romans 8:29-30; 1 Corinthians 1:8; Hebrews 6:4-6; Philippians 1:6

BELGIC CONFESSION

Article 24

PURPOSE

Pastor Lew begins today's video—the final video in Part One of this course—by telling about a woman who wondered if there was any hope for her husband, a new believer who had recently drifted away from God and the church. Pastor Lew then reviews the TULIP acronym, defining "perseverance of the saints" as the teaching that once you are a true believer, you will never fall away from God. He cites scriptural evidence supporting this doctrine of "eternal security," then contrasts it with the insecurity of "backsliding." Backsliding is part of what Pastor Lew calls the CURB set of beliefs held by some "free will" churches that emphasize the choices people make, as opposed to the choices God makes (the TULIP approach). CURB stands for **C**onditional election, **U**nlimited atonement, **R**esistable grace, and **B**acksliding. Unlike CURB, TULIP holds that we do not choose to remain in the kingdom of God, but that God keeps us there. In the difficult cases involving persons who have apparently drifted away from the faith, perhaps such persons were not believers in the first place or perhaps they will return to their faith later. But we should trust God to bring back all true believers. Pastor Lew concludes by talking about the wonderful security of knowing that God will always hang on to us in spite of our sins.

After today's session, your students should feel more secure, knowing that if they truly love God, he will hang on to them forever, come what may. Students should be able to define the doctrine of the perseverance of the saints and defend it from Scripture, contrast the beliefs represented by TULIP and CURB, and state what "perseverance of the saints" means to them personally.

PERSPECTIVE

The subject of this session is one of the most contested doctrines of the Reformed faith. It is challenged because many instances in the life of the church seem to contradict it. We teach that once saved, always saved; yet we know of some who have fallen away. So many people conclude that our doctrine must be wrong.

Not necessarily. There are answers to these seeming incongruities. Pastor Lew gives a few, and there are others. We begin with Hebrews 6, which seems to teach that a Christian can fall away and be lost. However, the writer of Scripture is not teaching here about falling away; rather, he warns us against remaining a babe in Christ. He urges us to grow into maturity (6:1). To strengthen his exhortation, he gives a hypothetical case of a person who has been blessed and then backslides, saying that such a one would be beyond hope. The analogy of land used in the next verses (7-8) is meant to teach that true faith, like good land, produces good fruit.

Verse 9 makes clear that the author is speaking hypothetically: "Even though we speak like this, dear friends, we are confident of better things in your case—things that accompany salvation."

Other passages also may seem to teach apostasy (1 Tim. 1:19-20; 2 Tim. 2:17-19), but all they say is that some who professed faith fell away later, or may fall away for a time. Whether their faith was true, or whether they were finally lost, is not stated. Warnings against apostasy and exhortations to continue in the way of faith and godliness are common in the New Testament. Since believers struggle in this life, these warnings are necessary and wholesome; they do not teach that true believers fall away.

Moreover, many passages teach the security of believers. Romans 8 is a whole chapter built around that theme. Romans 5:8-10 teaches that our standing as Christians is not based on our merits, for God reconciled us to himself while we were enemies because of our sin. Having done the greater work, he will do the lesser—having reconciled us, he will save us. Philippians 1:6 and John 6:39 are mentioned elsewhere in this lesson. Other passages speak about the gift of "eternal life" (John 3:16; 4:14; 5:24; 6:47, 51; 10:28; 1 John 5:11) or about the believers' union with Christ (John 14:19; Gal. 2:20) or about their names being written in heaven or the Lamb's book of life (Luke 10:20; Rev. 21:27).

All this Scripture teaches that salvation is a gift of God; God gives life and draws us to himself through the power of the Holy Spirit. He "is able to keep [us] from falling and to present [us] before his glorious presence without fault" (Jude 24). These passages must be interpreted in the context of the biblical doctrine of sovereign grace. The doctrine of the perseverance or preservation of the saints is part of a whole system of theology, all the parts of which must be accepted or rejected if we are consistent in our thinking. People dead in sin cannot animate themselves. God gives them life; God saves. Union with Christ, regeneration, conversion, and justification are unthinkable apart from salvation. Perseverance is inferred from these as well as expressly taught in Scripture. It means that God sustains and keeps those whom he has saved; theirs is an "inheritance that can never perish, spoil or fade—kept in heaven for [those] who through faith are shielded by God's power" until the completion of their salvation (1 Pet. 1:4-5; cf. 2 Tim. 1:12; 4:18).

This beautiful teaching, though sometimes misused by profane church members, assures believers of their salvation. Without assurance there is no joy; yet God says that the joy of his children should be full. Arminianism, which teaches the possibility of permanent falling away, has terrors which would cause me to shrink away from it forever, and which would fill me with constant and unspeakable perplexities. To feel that I were crossing the troubled and dangerous sea of life dependent for my final security upon the actings of my own treacherous nature were enough to fill me with perpetual alarm. If it is possible, I want to know that the vessel to which I commit my life is seaworthy, and that, once having embarked, I shall arrive in safety at my destination.

—Nathaniel S. McFetridge, *Calvinism in History,* p. 112

Sadly, some persons who once confessed Christ do fall away. Was their confession real? Were they truly engrafted into Christ? They may have been, and their falling away may have been the fault of the rest of us in the church—perhaps unfriendly, uncaring, unloving to those who need us. Perhaps we are the ones who do not have true faith. According to the Belgic Confession, "It is impossible for this holy faith to be unfruitful," for it is "faith working through love" (Article 24). As the video discussion guide notes, some may "slide over the edge" for a time and come back. Maybe we can help them come back. Others who fall away may never have known Christ. The apostle John was thinking of such men when he wrote:

> They went out from us, but they did not really belong to us. For if they had belonged to us, they would have remained with us; but their going showed that none of them belonged to us (1 John 2:19).

Many of your students may be dealing with their own spiritual doubts and uncertainties. This session on the perseverance of the saints presents an excellent opportunity to reassure them of the certainty of their salvation and of God's unfailing love for them.

PROCEDURE

Review Quiz

Before giving today's review quiz, you may want to ask students if they kept their commitment to do some helpful deed for someone during this past week (see Closing, session 11). Allow time for some comments.

1. true
2. false (sanctification is the cooperative work of the Holy Spirit and Christians)
3. false (our good works don't contribute anything to our salvation; we do them out of gratitude for what God has done for us)
4. true
5. true
6. false (faith and repentance are part of the conversion process)
7. true
8. false (God declares us not guilty on the basis of Christ's sacrifice on our behalf)
9. false (the first three steps are calling, regeneration, and conversion)
10. true

OPTION

For variety's sake, you may want to try a different kind of review quiz today. Give students about five minutes to make up five true/false statements of their own. Three of the statements should be based on last week's session about sanctification; two of the statements should be based on previous sessions. Students may use previous session guides, if available, but the questions should be their own. After writing their true/false statements, students should find a partner and ask their questions of each other.

TIP

Today's topic—eternal security in Christ—gives you an opportunity to help any of your teens who may be struggling with doubts about their faith. It is wonderfully comforting to know that, in spite of our doubts, in spite of who we are, in spite of our lapses into sin, God won't let us go. Watch for opportunities in this session to remind your group of this great truth. The option below is one such opportunity.

OPTION

Before showing today's video, mention that it's about something that can really help us as we deal with our spiritual doubts and with our struggles of faith. For example, maybe I'm wondering what kind of Christian I am, since I keep repeating the same sin or I really don't see any "good works" in my life. Or maybe I have some serious doubts and questions about God, or perhaps I just feel that my spiritual life is on hold.

Distribute notecards and invite those who wish to do so to jot down anything related to doubts/questions/struggles of faith. Be sure to complete a card yourself. Collect the (unsigned) cards and save them to use in responding to question 6. Ask the group to keep these doubts and questions in mind as they watch today's video.

Video Presentation

We suggest playing the video through without stopping.

Video Discussion Guide

1. **Review the differences between Calvinists and some "free will" churches, using the acronyms TULIP and CURB. Write a brief definition behind each letter.**

   Help your students recall the definitions of each word in the acronyms, contrasting the two views at each point:

   T Total depravity. Every aspect of our being is tainted with sin.

   U Unconditional election. God's choice to save some of the human race.

   L Limited atonement. Jesus died for the elect, not for everyone.

   I Irresistible grace. Once God's Spirit begins working in our hearts, we can't turn away.

   P Perseverance of the saints. Once we believe, we will never fall away from God. Louis Berkhof offers this more complete definition: "Perseverance is that continuous operation of the Holy Spirit in the believer, by which the work of divine grace that is begun in the heart, is continued and brought to completion"(*Manual of Christian Doctrine*).

   Note: There's no "T" in the CURB acronym. However, the free-will view of total depravity is basically the same as the Calvinist approach.

   C Conditional election. God's electing love is based on our acceptance and belief.

   U Unlimited atonement. Jesus died for everyone, not just the elect.

   R Resistible grace. We have the ability to say no to God's Spirit working in our hearts.

   B Backsliding. We can lose our salvation even if we are true Christians.

2. **Read the following passages that support the idea that God will never let us go: John 6:37-40; Romans 8:29-30; 1 Corinthians 1:8; Philippians 1:6. Which passage speaks most clearly and powerfully to you about your "eternal security" in Christ?**

   Let your students read these passages to themselves, pick one, then read that passage aloud to the class and tell why they picked it. Summaries of each passage follow:

   - John 6:37-40 quotes Jesus, who says he came to get the ones the Father elected and that he (Jesus) will lose none of the elect.
   - Romans 8:29-30 weaves an unbreakable chain from God's election to God's glorification of those who believe in him.

- 1 Corinthians 1:8 says that God will preserve us, blameless, to the end of time.
- Philippians 1:6 says that God will finish the good work he began in us.

3. Doesn't the saying "Once a Christian, always a Christian" contradict Hebrews 6:4-6, which says that it is impossible for those who "have once been enlightened" and who have fallen away to be brought back to repentance? Explain.

Read this passage with your students; then do a bit of reflecting on its meaning. Certainly those who do not believe in "eternal security" take this passage to mean that Christians can actually lose their faith. However, the passage can be interpreted in several other ways. One interpretation, given by Pastor Lew, argues that the passage refers to the impossibility of wandering Christians returning to God *on their own*—only God can bring them back. Another interpretation (see the Perspective section of this session) views the passage as a hypothetical argument to warn spiritually immature Christians to "grow up" spiritually. A third interpretation holds that the passage is talking about people who were never true Christians in the first place. According to the *NIV Study Bible* notes on the passage, such persons "had come under the influence of God's covenant blessings and had professed to turn from darkness to light but were in danger of a public and final rejection of Christ, proving that they had never been regenerated."

4. One objection to believing the saying "Once a Christian, always a Christian" is that it could lead to a kind of "lazy" Christianity in which people pretty much do as they please, since they're saved anyway. How would you respond to this?

The doctrine of the perseverance of the saints doesn't make for lazy Christians because true Christians love God enough to want to do their best for him. Christians view obedience and other spiritual activities as acts of love, not chores.

5. A friend of yours confides that her older brother, John, has lost all interest in Christianity. He used to be very active in the church and was a strong Christian. But after he got married, he rarely went to church, and now he says he no longer believes in Jesus. Her parents are very upset about the situation and pray daily for him. Your friend is worried about her brother. She wonders what you think about the situation.

a. Does this example contradict the doctrine of the perseverance of the saints? Why or why not?

b. What would you say to your friend?

The example of John does not contradict the doctrine of the perseverance of the saints. One tragic possibility is that John was not a true Christian in the first

OPTION

Also read the last two sections of Article 28 of the Belgic Confession with the group. These sections remind us that we must trust God's grace or live in doubt and uncertainty. We can't do anything to get ourselves into the kingdom of heaven and we can't do anything to keep ourselves there either. God, who gets us there in the first place, is not going to let us go.

TIP

Looking closely at the Hebrews passage with your group gives you an opportunity to recall some of the Bible-study techniques taught earlier in this course. Do your students remember S.I.S.—the principle of Scripture interpreting Scripture? In interpreting this passage we need to remember that many other passages in Scripture teach the principle of eternal security or perseverance of the saints.

TIP

Bring in some Bible-study tools (*NIV Study Bible,* commentaries) and let students use them to arrive at their own interpretation of the passage.

place; perhaps his faith was not genuine. Another possibility is that God may be allowing John to temporarily "slide over the edge," only to rescue him later, after he's recognized his need for the Father.

OPTION

Break into small groups to discuss this question. Have groups outline their responses, then, if time allows, ask the groups to report their conclusions to the class.

In responding to such a situation, we ought to recognize the second possibility. As Pastor Lew suggests, we need to be careful not to be judgmental—it's best to accept a person's profession to be a Christian as genuine. Accepting the second possibility—of a temporary "slide over the edge"—means that we should never give up hope that God will find a way to bring him home to himself. We can trust God to do that because God says so in the Bible. Meanwhile, we should do everything in our power to help bring John back into the church. One important and comforting thing we can do in such a situation is to offer to pray for the person who is drifting.

OPTION

If you had students list their doubts and struggles on notecards (see earlier option), this is the time to read those cards aloud. Talk about the comfort we have in knowing that our salvation is secure, even in the midst of our doubts and struggles.

6. **Reflect on your feelings about the saying "Once a Christian, always a Christian." When would knowing this be especially comforting to you?**

Give your students time to think, then ask for responses. We hope that at least some students will talk about the solid comfort of knowing that once God has hold of us, it doesn't matter what circumstances we face, because ultimately God will lead us to glory. This is especially comforting to know when we feel far from God because of our sins, when we're going through some crisis, or when we feel generally depressed and down.

Closing

OPTION

Psalm 46 reminds us that "God is our refuge and strength, an ever-present help in time of trouble." Read this psalm responsively as part of your closing devotions.

Ask your group to close their eyes and listen as you read the comforting words of Jesus found in John 6:37-40. Then offer a brief prayer of thanks that Jesus will never drive us away. He will not lose any of us, and one day he will bring us to heaven to be with him.

Note: If you will be ending your study of *What We Believe* with this session, you may want to take some time to talk with your students about what they liked and disliked about the course. And please pass your comments along to us. You can reach us at 1-800-333-8300 or e-mail us at editors@crcpublications.org.

If you're continuing on to Part Two (sessions 13-24) of the course, be sure you have the new leader's guide, the session guides, and the videocassettes ready to use.